LawExpress
EQUITY AND TRUSTS

EQUITY AND TRUSTS

LawExpress

7th edition

John Duddington
Former Head of the Law School, Worcester College of Technology
Lecturer in Law, University of Worcester

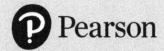 **Pearson**

Harlow, England • London • New York • Boston • San Francisco • Toronto • Sydney • Dubai • Singapore • Hong Kong
Tokyo • Seoul • Taipei • New Delhi • Cape Town • São Paulo • Mexico City • Madrid • Amsterdam • Munich • Paris • Milan

PEARSON EDUCATION LIMITED
KAO Two
KAO Park
Harlow CM17 9NA
United Kingdom
Tel: +44 (0)1279 623623
Web: www.pearson.com/uk

First published 2007 (print and electronic)
Second edition published 2009 (print and electronic)
Third edition published 2011 (print and electronic)
Fourth edition published 2013 (print and electronic)
Fifth edition published 2014 (print and electronic)
Sixth edition published 2017 (print and electronic)
Seventh edition published 2019 (print and electronic)

Contains public sector information licensed under the Open Government Licence (OGL) v3.0.
http://www.nationalarchives.gov.uk/doc/open-government-licence/version/3/

Contains Parliamentary information licensed under the Open Parliament Licence (OPL) v3.0.
http://www.parliament.uk/site-information/copyright/open-parliament-licence/

Pearson Education is not responsible for the content of third-party internet sites.

ISBN: 978-1-292-21017-9 (print)
       978-1-292-21069-8 (PDF)
       978-1-292-21050-6 (ePub)

British Library Cataloguing-in-Publication Data
A catalogue record for the print edition is available from the British Library

10 9 8 7 6 5 4 3
23 22 21 20 19

Print edition typeset in 10/12pt Helvetica Neue LT W1G by Spi Global
Printed and bound in Great Britain by Ashford Colour Press Ltd

NOTE THAT ANY PAGE CROSS REFERENCES REFER TO THE PRINT EDITION

Contents

Acknowledgements

Writing Law Express books has now become part of my life and so my thanks go to those who share that life: my wife Anne, for her constant support, loyalty and technical expertise, without which my books would never begin to be written; my daughter Mary, for her seemingly faultless proofreading and sense of fun which keeps me going; and my son Christopher, for just being himself. In addition, I can never forget my father, Walter Duddington, who first encouraged me to become a lawyer, and who would, I am sure, have been an equity enthusiast.

I would also like to thank the staff of Pearson Education for their encouragement, cheerfulness and practical guidance, and the reviewers who sent in such detailed and helpful suggestions for this edition.

Equity and trusts is a fast-moving area and, once again, there have been developments in virtually every topic in this book since the previous edition. There have been significant cases on such areas as certainty of intention to create a trust, *donatio mortis causa,* secret trusts, trusts of the family home and breach of trust, to name only some. Indeed, I have made changes to virtually all chapters to reflect both legal developments and examination practice. Moreover, it is gratifying to see so much scholarly writing taking place on equity and trusts; it also means that students must, for a good mark, keep up with this and I have given references to some of these writings in the hope that students will explore further.

The book is based on materials available to me on the day it was completed: 12 October 2017 which, by a happy chance, is also my birthday!

John Duddington

Former Head of the Law School, Worcester College of Technology
Lecturer in Law, University of Worcester

Publisher's acknowledgements

Our thanks go to all reviewers who contributed to the development of this text, including students who participated in research and focus groups which helped to shape the series format.

Introduction

■ Some general issues

Most students achieve an average mark in equity exams, some do not pass at all, and others do very well. So far this is typical of all exams, but in my experience the number of students who do very well is smaller than in other law exams. Why? This introduction aims to give you some pointers to getting into the category of those who do very well, and equally pointers for simply achieving a pass. What are the problems that students commonly face in tackling these questions? How does this guide help?

It is not a superficial guide which skims the surface of the subject but it aims to help you in the following ways:

- It provides a platform for the study of equity by taking you through the fundamental areas step by step and encourages you not to go on to the next area until you have mastered the one before.
- It links different areas by revision notes which clearly point you to other connected areas of the syllabus.
- It highlights key cases, statutes and definitions.
- It gives you tips for the exam based on my experience over 30 years as an equity and trusts examiner.
- It shows you how each topic develops by a visual map attached to each chapter.
- It gives you suggestions for further reading which will enable you to boost your exam marks.

What this guide *cannot* do is to:

- Do away with the need to learn the material thoroughly and be able to use it in the exam. Only you can do this!
- Act as a substitute for the standard textbooks.

■ General essay question advice

Equity is founded on a number of doctrines such as the concept of a fiduciary, unconscionability, notice and discretion in the grant of remedies. Students often simply scratch the surface when discussing these and this is the major reason why they do essay questions badly.

Take the concept of a fiduciary.

This is relevant in questions on constructive trusts, trustees, the nature of equity and undue influence. As such it is very well worth knowing some ideas of precisely what it means. But take a typical answer to this question:

'The concept of a fiduciary is at the heart of equity.'
What do you understand by the term 'fiduciary' and to what extent is this true?

This appears to be relatively easy. Students can remember cases in which the fiduciary concept has been relevant and they put them together. I have read hundreds of answers like this. Cases such as *Keech* v *Sandford* (1726) and *Boardman* v *Phipps* (1967) are dealt with and, in each instance, it is remarked that they are examples of the fiduciary principle. Possibly *Queensland Mines Ltd* v *Hudson* (1978) is mentioned as an example of where the fiduciary principle did not apply.

This is leading to a mark of around 50 per cent. There is knowledge of the case law and students will be surprised that they have not done better in spite of all their work. The reason is simple: they have just scratched the surface. No attempt has been made to deal with the nature of the fiduciary concept. What is it about? A good answer would explain that the central idea is that of loyalty, which then translates into a principle that the fiduciary must not allow a conflict of interest between their duties as a fiduciary and their personal interests. How do fiduciary relationships arise? Is it through a voluntary undertaking on the part of the fiduciary? Moreover, the above examples of fiduciary relationships refer only to trustees. What about undue influence? Remember to take examples from as wide an area as possible. (Fiduciaries are mainly dealt with in Chapter 8 (for constructive trusts) and Chapter 2 (for undue influence).) In addition, remember to refer to scholarly writing on this area.

A student intervenes at this point: How can I cover all the cases *and* deal with the theoretical issues?

Answer: you cannot, so you will not be penalised for not doing so. Select a few cases, learn them well, read around them and relate them to the theoretical issues you have discussed. You will now be on the way to a good pass. *Less detail – more depth.*

◼ General problem question advice

These are easier as the structure of the problem gives you the structure of your answer. However, in equity problems there are often rather subtle points which, when picked up, can give you extra marks. A good example is secret and half-secret trusts (see Chapter 6), a very common area for problems.

Here is one example. The generally accepted rule for communication of a half-secret trust is that the details of the trust must be communicated before the will (*Re Keen* (1937)). However, *Re Keen* is also authority for another rule which can conflict with this: that the details must be communicated in accordance with the terms of the will. Again, an answer which scores about 50 per cent will mention and apply the first rule, which is probably the correct one. However, an answer which also applies the other rule will clearly score more. (These rules are all dealt with in Chapter 6.)

Another subtle point arising here is the law where the trust is communicated to one trustee but not the other. Is the one to whom it is not communicated bound? (See *Re Stead* (1900).) Learn these rather tricky points thoroughly.

◼ About this book

This book is *not* a potted version of the subject. You will not find within it all the detail you need to pass your exams. It is an aid to learning and not a substitute to reading textbooks, articles (essential if you want a good pass) and, of course, attendance at lectures, tutorials and seminars. It can be used either at the end of the course as a revision aid or during the course to guide you along. Above all it tries to encourage you to *think* about the subject. Thinking students are those who gain the highest marks in exams.

Journals referred to in the 'Read to impress' sections are as follows:

ALJ	*Australian Law Journal*
All ER Review	*All England Law Review*
CLJ	*Cambridge Law Journal*
Conv.	*Conveyancer and Property Lawyer*
LQR	*Law Quarterly Review*
LS	*Legal Studies*
MLR	*Modern Law Review*
SLT	*Scots Law Times*

📖 **REVISION NOTE**

Success in exams in equity and trusts requires the following:

- an ability to tackle essay questions in such areas as the nature of equity, constructive trusts and equitable remedies;
- an ability to tackle complex problem questions in areas such as constitution of trusts, charities and secret trusts;
- dealing with theoretical concepts (usually at the start of your answer);
- using a wide range of examples.

Throughout your revision, use the questions on the companion website to check your understanding of the subject, and to identify areas where you may want to focus your revision.

✎ **EXAM TIP**

Do keep up to date especially with case law in this area. For example, during the currency of this edition, there will be significant case law and statutory developments in many of the areas covered by this book.

Guided tour

How to use features in the book 📖 and the companion **website** 🖱

Understand quickly

Topic maps – Visual guides highlight key subject areas and facilitate easy navigation through the chapter. Download them from the companion website to pin on your wall or add to your revision notes.

Key definitions – Make sure you understand essential legal terms.

Key cases and key statutes – Identify and review the important elements of the essential cases and statutes you will need to know for your exams.

Read to impress – These carefully selected sources will extend your knowledge, deepen your understanding, and help you to earn better marks in coursework and exams.

Glossary – Forgotten the meaning of a word? This quick reference covers key definitions and other useful terms.

Test your knowledge – How well do you know each topic? Test yourself with quizzes tailored specifically to each chapter.

Revise effectively

Revision checklists – Identify essential points you should know for your exams. The chapters will help you revise each point to ensure you are fully prepared. Print the checklists from the companion website to track your progress.

Revision notes – These boxes highlight related points and areas where your course might adopt a particular approach that you should check with your course tutor.

Flashcards – Test and improve recall of important legal terms, key cases and statutes. Available in both electronic and printable formats.

Take exams with confidence

Sample questions with answer guidelines – Practice makes perfect! Consider how you would answer the question at the start of each chapter then refer to answer guidance at the end of the chapter. Try out additional sample questions online.

Assessment advice – Use this feature to identify how a subject may be examined and how to apply your knowledge effectively.

Make your answer stand out – Impress your examiners with these sources of further thinking and debate.

Exam tips – Feeling the pressure? These boxes indicate how you can improve your exam performance when it really counts.

Don't be tempted to – Spot common pitfalls and avoid losing marks.

You be the marker – Evaluate sample exam answers and understand how and why an examiner awards

Table of cases

Cases

TABLE OF CASES

Legislation

Nature of equity and trusts

1

Revision checklist

Essential points you should know:

- [ ] The meanings of the term 'equity'
- [ ] The reasons why equity developed as a separate system of law
- [ ] What is meant by the concept of a trust
- [ ] The later development of equity in outline
- [ ] The modern arguments for and against whether equity and the common law are now fused

■ Topic map

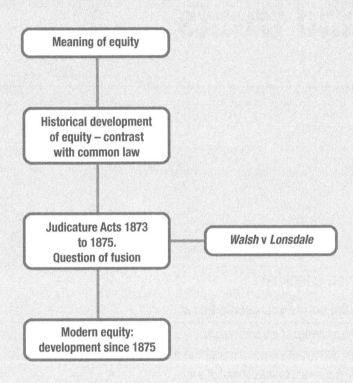

■ Introduction

This chapter is perhaps the most important in this book.

However, unlike all other chapters, it does not contain all the material needed to answer an examination question.

The reason is that this chapter sets the scene for a study of equity and, in addition to guiding you on the meanings of the term 'equity' and the history of its development, it points you in the direction of various themes in the study of equity. The detail on some of these will be found in later chapters. The answer to any question on the nature and/ or development of equity will obviously require an essay. This is one area where it is absolutely essential to read beyond the standard textbooks in order to gain an above-average pass and this chapter points you in the direction of a variety of additional reading in the 'Make your answer stand out' sections.

There is also a separate section on the development of the trust and the uses to which trusts can be put today. This often forms the subject of an exam question and, again, this section points you in the direction of themes which are picked up in more depth in later chapters.

ASSESSMENT ADVICE

An essay question can take one of these forms:

- The historical development of equity. This would be less likely than the other possibilities.

- The relationship between equity and the common law. This is the most likely area, as it will involve you looking at the distinctive features of equity and contrasting them with the common law. There is an opportunity to use your knowledge of other areas (e.g. contract and tort) when you discuss the common law, and this will gain extra marks.

- The possibility of equity and the common law converging in the future. This is an area on which a good deal has been written recently, so you need to have read widely in order to be able to answer it well. On the whole, it is not dealt with in much depth in standard textbooks.

- The uses to which trusts can be put, with an emphasis on their versatility.

Two other points:

- It is possible for a question to cover all these issues; for example, it may ask you to analyse the reasons why equity developed, how significant it is today, and how it may develop in the future.

▶

> ■ Be careful to check whether the question asks you to discuss 'modern equity'. 'Modern' really means since the Judicature Acts, so no credit will be given for historical material. It is a common error among students to feel that they must include historical material whatever the question asks. Resist it!

■ Sample question

Could you answer this question? Below is a typical essay question that could arise on this topic. Guidelines on answering the question are included at the end of this chapter, while another sample essay question and guidance on tackling it can be found on the companion website.

ESSAY QUESTION

'The courts in their equitable jurisdiction have more scope for developing the law in a conscionable manner than they have in their common law jurisdiction.'

(Hayton and Mitchell, 2010)

Evaluate this statement by reference to the growth and development of modern equity.

■ Meaning of equity

Equity has various meanings. In a general sense, equity means fairness or justice. However, this is too general on its own for law exams and it also takes us into a wider debate about what precisely 'fairness' and 'justice' mean. Instead we need to:

- consider the term 'conscience': this has a long history in equity – the Chancellor was known as the Keeper of the King's Conscience;
- consider recent cases where the courts have used the term 'unconscionability', which at least is derived from conscience (see, e.g., *Pennington* v *Waine* (2002) in Chapter 5);
- make it clear that equity today does not mean the same as justice in the broad sense;
- contrast equity with other terms (e.g. charity and mercy);
- consider and apply the principle that equity may intervene where the application of a strict rule of law would cause injustice (e.g. it might allow a mortgage to be redeemed even though the actual redemption date had passed);
- state that, in the legal sense, equity means the body of principles developed by the Court of Chancery.

Make your answer stand out

You will certainly improve your mark in an essay question on the nature of equity if you read beyond the standard textbooks in this area. A good place to start is Watt (2009), especially pages 36–41 on 'Multiple meanings of equity'. Even better would be to read (or see!) Shakespeare's *Measure for Measure,* which has a lot to say on these themes.

In an essay on the nature of equity you could then discuss the characteristics of equity: it is discretionary, it acts as a supplement to the common law (not a complete system on its own), it acts *in personam,* etc.

For all these points you need examples drawn from equity and this is a good opportunity to show your wide knowledge.

KEY CASE

Patel v *Ali* [1984] Ch 283 (HC)

Concerning: principles for the grant of an equitable remedy

Facts

A contract was made for the sale of a house but during a long delay in going on to completion the seller had a leg amputated and she gave birth to her second and third children. This meant that she came to rely on help from friends and relatives. The buyers sought **specific performance** (SP) (equitable remedy) to compel the seller to complete.

Legal principle

SP would be refused as there would be hardship amounting to injustice if it was granted because the seller would lose the help on which she relied if she was forced to move.

Patel v *Ali* is an excellent case on which to build part of an answer on the nature of equity. It shows that:

- equitable remedies are discretionary – common law remedies are not. The seller would have to pay damages (common law remedy) for her breach of the contract of sale;
- equity is not just a question of the court exercising a complete discretion: there are certain principles on which it exercises a discretion. In the above case the court emphasised that to compel the seller to move would amount to 'hardship amounting to injustice'. The normal rule is that SP is granted in contracts for the sale of land where the seller fails to complete; in this case the rule was displaced.

An exam question often asks if equity is just a matter of the court in each case having complete discretion. Although discretion means much more than this, you will need to say that some judges do give the impression that equity is just individual discretion on their part – see below.

📖 **REVISION NOTE**

Chapter 2 contains a number of other cases on specific performance which you can use in an answer in conjunction with *Patel* v *Ali*.

✓ Make your answer stand out

You should research the term 'unconscionability'. It can be argued that, although the term is valuable as a general pointer to the direction to which equity should take, it is of no use as a practical tool in the application of equitable principles. Consider this point and read Hopkins (2006), who considers the utility of unconscionability as a rationale for equitable intervention.

Figure 1.1

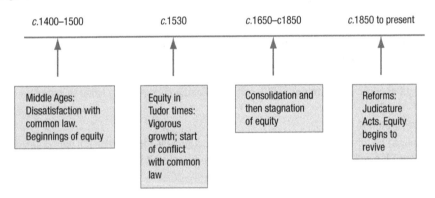

Exam questions are not likely to ask you just for a historical account of equity and so you should look at the history to see whether it gives pointers to how equity operates today, which is a much more likely area for a question.

■ Maxims of equity

These are signposts to how equitable jurisdiction might be exercised, but they are not fixed rules. Examples (and where illustrations on their application may be found in this book) are:

- equity looks to the intent and not the form (Chapters 5 and 6);
- equity will not allow a statute to be used as an instrument of fraud (Chapters 6 and 8);
- equity will not assist a volunteer (Chapter 5).

Look at how equity developed as a supplement to the common law (e.g. by using remedies such as injunctions and SP to prevent injustice) and then mention that this is still the case today (e.g. the modern *Mareva* (freezing) and *Anton Piller* (search) orders which are examples of injunctions (see Chapter 2)).

Look at how the maxims of equity gradually developed and then give examples of how these are still used today.

✓ Make your answer stand out

Tinsley v *Milligan* (1994) is an excellent example of how the Court of Appeal and the House of Lords both used the maxim 'he who comes to equity must come with clean hands' but applied it differently (see Chapter 7).

You should also look at how **trusts** were originally used and at how the trust concept has now developed.

Development of the trust

You may not get questions on the historical development of the trust but you should use this chapter to make sure that you are absolutely clear on the following fundamental points.

What is a trust?

Key Definition: Trust

This is a relationship that arises when property is vested in a person (or persons) called the trustees, which those trustees are obliged to hold for the benefit of other persons called the *cestuis que trust* or beneficiaries (Hanbury and Martin (2015: 41)).

Who is the settlor?

KEY DEFINITION: Settlor

The creator of the trust which is created by the settlor transferring property to the trustees to hold on trust or alternatively declaring that he/she is the trustee. If the trust is created by will then the trust is created by the testator.

Who are the beneficiaries?

KEY DEFINITION: Beneficiaries

Those for whom the property is held on trust and who therefore have an equitable interest in the property.

The idea that the **beneficiaries** have an equitable interest in the trust property is one of the concepts at the heart of equity. It underlies cases such as *Barclays Bank Ltd* v *Quistclose Investments Ltd* (1970) (see Chapter 7). The effect is that in equity the beneficiaries own the trust property, and if it is wrongly taken from the trust the beneficiaries are in a better position than creditors who have to claim the return of money owed to them as a debt, as they can use the remedies set out in Chapter 12.

Suppose that someone has purchased the trust property. Can the beneficiaries reclaim it from them? This brings us to another definition.

KEY DEFINITION: Notice

A purchaser is bound by an equitable interest unless he/she had either actual notice of the equitable interest of the beneficiaries, or constructive notice or imputed notice.

- Actual **notice** means actual knowledge.
- Constructive notice means that the purchaser should have been aware of the equitable interest had reasonable enquiries been made.
- Imputed notice means that if the agent or employee of the purchaser had notice, then the purchaser will also have notice.

📖 REVISION NOTE

If you are studying land law, or have studied it, then go back to your land law materials and check what it says on notice. See *Land Law* in the *Law Express* series, especially Chapters 1 and 2.

Take this exam question: 'In the complexity of modern society there are many activities which depend of the concept of the trust.' This is an example of a type of question that you need to be prepared for which is not too difficult but which does require thought and preparation. Have it in mind when you are reading this book and then make a list of areas where the trust plays a vital part: trusts where there is a will, trusts of the home, charities, trusts for clubs and societies, etc. Then research this area and bring in other areas such as trusts for pension funds and trusts where land is left to someone under age. This point is dealt with fully in one of the answers on the companion website.

▌Judicature Acts 1873 and 1875 and the question of fusion

The Judicature Acts abolished both the old common law courts and the Court of Chancery and replaced them with a new Supreme Court consisting of the High Court and the Court of Appeal. The Judicature Act 1873 provided that where equity and the common law conflict, then equity shall prevail (s. 25(11)). The passage of this Act led to a debate which is still not settled on the extent to which equity and the common law are fused.

The question of whether equity and the common law are, or are not, fused is a very familiar area for exam questions. It is an issue that is still debated and so there is no right answer – do not feel that you have to come to one.

Fusion can mean two things:

1   That the *administration* of equity and the common law is fused. This means that all divisions of the High Court have jurisdiction in both common law and equity, unlike before when only the Court of Chancery exercised equitable jurisdiction.

2   That the actual systems of common law and equity have been fused so that it is no longer correct to speak of common law and equity, but of one system. This aspect has given rise to debate. Lord Diplock in *United Scientific Holdings* v *Burnley BC* (1978) considered that law and equity are fused, in contrast to the well-known statement of Ashburner in *Principles of Equity* (1933), who compared law and equity to separate streams which, although running side by side, 'do not mingle their waters'. In fact, there has been a vigorous growth in equity since the middle years of the twentieth century. See, for example, the fiduciary concept (Chapter 8), the law on trusts of the home (Chapter 8) and equitable remedies and doctrines (Chapter 2).

When reading this book, make a note of the areas where equity's intervention has been more marked (as indicated above) as this could form the basis of an answer on equity. Try to include examples from as wide a range as possible. This is dealt with in more detail below.

As an alternative, exam questions may ask you to consider whether common law and equity ought to exist as separate systems of law.

 Make your answer stand out

You should be aware of the debate on the future of equity as a separate system, and whether it is necessary to regard equitable and common law jurisdiction as distinct. Sarah Worthington, in her book *Equity* (2006), argues strongly for the end of two distinct systems. She points out that the origin of equity is to be found in history and not policy. This is unarguable, but it is easy to forget that it is so. For a view that trusts do not need to exist under a system of equitable duties and rights, see Honoré (2003).

What is clear is that the Judicature Acts did fuse the administration of law and equity.

KEY CASE

Walsh v *Lonsdale* (1882) 21 Ch D 9 (HC)

Concerning: effect of the Judicature Acts

Facts

A lease was granted but not by deed. Thus, it was only equitable – an agreement for a lease can be enforced by equity on the basis of the maxim that 'equity looks on that as done which ought to be done', i.e. if a person has agreed to grant a lease then that person ought to do so and, as far as possible, equity will assume that they have done so.

Legal principle

The court applied section 25(11) of the Judicature Act 1873 and held that, as equity prevailed, there was an equitable lease.

Modern equity – developments since 1875

This is a likely area for exam questions and you will find the following chapters particularly useful:

- Chapter 2: equitable remedies and doctrines.
- Chapters 7 and 8: resulting trusts and constructive trusts – especially thinking about how the constructive trust can be used.
- Chapter 8: the section on trusts of the home – the extent to which equity has recognised rights here has been one of the best modern examples of equity.

Note also the following:

- The extent to which equity is flourishing in Australia (e.g. see *Queensland Mines Ltd* v *Hudson* (1978) in Chapter 8).
- In various cases judges are starting to base their decisions on wider grounds (e.g. unconscionability) – see, for example, *Pennington* v *Waine* (2002) in Chapter 5.
- How judges often today seem more forward looking than, for example, judges in the 1950s (e.g. see the judgments of Lord Simonds in a number of charity cases in Chapter 9, such as *Oppenheim* v *Tobacco Securities Trust Co. Ltd* (1951) and *Gilmour* v *Coats* (1949)).

Putting it all together

Answer guidelines

See the essay question at the start of this chapter.

Approaching the question

You need to select no more than four areas and look at the contribution of equity and consider the term 'conscionable'. Never make the mistake of trying to say something about everything: you will end up by saying nothing worthwhile about anything!

Important points to include

This is up to you as long as you make sure that:

- you relate the points you make to the question;
- you link them to each other so that the essay has a theme.

Some ideas on what to include are:

- Trusts of the family home. How did equity intervene? What did it do that the common law could not have done?

▶

■ Secret trusts. Obviously, the common law would not have enforced these – explain why. Do not just explain what a secret trust is but say why you feel it is/is not right that equity should enforce them.

■ Constructive trusts. Same approach as with secret trusts; take a case such as *Boardman* v *Phipps* (1967) – consider the response of the common law and then that of equity. Here you have an interesting point as it could be argued that in this case equity set the standard of the trustee's fiduciary duty too high. Learn some key phrases from both the majority and dissenting judgments in the House of Lords and integrate them into your answer.

 ## Make your answer stand out

End by referring to the debate about the place of equity – although it may have made a great contribution in the past, is there a need for it today? Does the common law recognise issues of conscience? Is it capable of doing so?

READ TO IMPRESS

Ashburner, W. (1933) *Principles of Equity,* 2nd edn. London: Butterworths.

Duddington, J. (2014) Blueprints series: *Equity and Trusts.* Harlow: Pearson Education, especially Ch. 1.

Hanbury, G. and Martin, J. (2015) *Modern Equity,* (Glister J. and Lee J. eds.) 20th edn. London: Sweet and Maxwell.

Hayton, D. and Mitchell, O. (2010) *The Law of Trusts and Equitable Remedies,* 13th edn. London: Sweet and Maxwell.

Honoré, T. (2003) Trusts, the inessentials, in Getzler, J. (ed.) *Rationalising Property, Equity and Trusts: Essays in Honour of Edward Burn.* London: Lexis Nexis.

Hopkins, N. (2006) Conscience, discretion and the creation of property rights. 26 *LS* 475.

Mason, A. (1994) The place of equity and equitable remedies in the common law world. 110 *LQR* 238.

Watt, G. (2009) *Equity Stirring: The Story of Justice Beyond Law.* Oxford: Hart Publishing.

Worthington, S. (2006) *Equity,* 2nd edn. Oxford: Oxford University Press.

www.pearsoned.co.uk/lawexpress

 Go online to access more revision support including quizzes to test your knowledge, sample questions with answer guidelines, printable versions of the topic maps, and more!

Equitable
remedies
and doctrines

2

Revision checklist

Essential points you should know:

- [ ] The characteristics of equitable remedies
- [ ] The situations in which a grant of the remedies of injunction, specific performance, rescission and rectification would be appropriate
- [ ] The meaning of 'undue influence'
- [ ] The situations when undue influence is presumed and when it is not
- [ ] The effect of undue influence (and misrepresentation) on third parties

■ Topic map

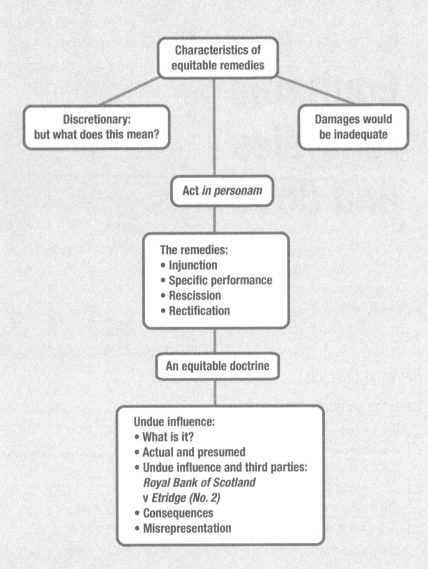

◼ Introduction

This is not a difficult topic but you should check whether your syllabus includes it.

If your syllabus specifies only study of the law of trusts it will probably not include equity as a separate area. However, syllabuses for those courses where the final qualification gives exemption from the academic stage of qualifying as a barrister or solicitor (i.e. a qualifying law degree) must include equity other than trusts, and so it is almost certain that you will be examined on equity as such.

ASSESSMENT ADVICE

Essay questions

An essay will often deal with equitable remedies and may ask you to consider them in the light of a particular quotation. This should not pose great problems of understanding; rather, the problem is often the amount of material to hand and the consequent danger of simply ploughing through it with no real attempt to answer the question. The golden rule applies: make a selection of material and use it to address the issues raised in the question. Nothing more! Other possibilities are essays on undue influence, especially the decision in *Barclays Bank plc* v *O'Brien* (1994) and subsequent cases.

Problem questions

Problem questions are less likely on the remedies, although possible questions could be asked on specific performance, freezing and/or search orders.

A more likely area is undue influence where there are various issues to explore, and this is the area chosen for a problem question on the companion website to this chapter.

◼ Sample question

Could you answer this question? Below is a typical essay question that could arise on this topic. Guidelines on answering the question are included at the end of this chapter, while a sample problem question and guidance on tackling it can be found on the companion website.

'Equitable remedies are discretionary.'

Do you agree?

Characteristics of equitable remedies

1. *They are discretionary,* whereas the common law remedy of damages is available as of right. This does not mean, however, that everything is left to the discretion of the court in each case: as we shall see, there are clear principles governing the grant of equitable remedies.

2. *They are granted where the common law remedies (e.g. damages) would be inadequate* or where the common law remedies are not available because the right is exclusively equitable (e.g. a right of a beneficiary under a trust).

3. *They act in personam,* i.e. against the defendant personally.

Points (1) and (2) are illustrated by the case of *Patel* v *Ali* (1984).

📖 **REVISION NOTE**

Go back to Chapter 1 and check that you are familiar with the *Patel* v *Ali* case. It is an excellent illustration of equitable remedies.

In *Patel* v *Ali* (1984) you can see that equitable remedies, although discretionary, are not granted at the whim of the court: note the phrase 'hardship amounting to injustice' as the principle here. Note this quote from *Vercoe and others* v *Rutland Fund Management Ltd and others* (2010): 'Although in a certain sense the courts' decisions about these matters might be described as discretionary, in truth I think the courts are now seeking to articulate underlying principles which will govern the choices to be made as to the remedy or remedies available in any given case.'

The next section will look at the main remedies.

Injunctions

An **injunction** may be used:

- to restrain a breach of contract;
- to restrain the commission of a tort (e.g. a nuisance or a trespass);
- to restrain a breach of confidence;
- to restrain a breach of trust;
- in matrimonial and family matters. (The Family Law Act 1996 gives the courts extensive powers to grant injunctions in divorce proceedings.)

> **KEY DEFINITION: Injunction**
>
> This is a court order requiring a party either to do or not to do a particular act.

Perpetual injunctions

Perpetual injunctions will not necessarily last for ever but they are final in that they will finally resolve the issue between the parties. There are two types of perpetual injunction:

1. *Prohibitory,* i.e. restraining the doing of an act.
2. *Mandatory,* i.e. commanding the doing of an act.

Interlocutory injunctions

The object of an interlocutory injunction is to preserve the status quo until the trial of an action – for example, to restrain an association from holding a meeting without allowing certain members to attend (*Woodford* v *Smith* (1970)).

They may be:

- prohibitory (see above);
- mandatory (see above); or
- *quia timet.*

A *quia timet* injunction is granted to restrain a threatened apprehended injury to the claimant's rights even though no injury has yet occurred. For example, in *Torquay Hotel Co. Ltd* v *Cousins* (1969) the defendants, members of a trade union, intended to picket the claimant's hotel to prevent the delivery of fuel oil that would interfere with the execution of contracts which the claimants had made for the supply of that oil. A *quia timet* injunction was granted.

Interlocutory injunctions are often granted without notice to the other side – the old term for this was *ex parte.*

Principles on the grant of interlocutory injunctions

KEY CASE

American Cyanamid Co. v *Ethicon Ltd (No 1)* [1975] AC 396 (HL)

Concerning: principles on which an interlocutory injunction will be granted

Facts

There was an application for a *quia timet* injunction to prevent the infringement of a patent.

Legal principles

The court laid down the following principles to be followed when deciding to grant an interlocutory injunction:

(a) Is there a serious question to be tried? If the defendant has no arguable defence at all then an injunction will be granted and points (b) and (c) below do not arise. Otherwise the court will consider the following points.

(b) If there is a serious issue, will damages be an adequate remedy so that an injunction will not be needed? This must be looked at from the point of view of:

    (i) The claimant, i.e. would damages be adequate compensation for loss caused to him by acts of the defendant before the trial?

    (ii) The defendant, i.e. if the claimant loses at the trial, then could any loss to the defendant be compensated by the claimant giving an undertaking in damages?

(c) If damages would be inadequate, then should an injunction be granted taking into account the balance of convenience to each party? *Hubbard* v *Pitt* (1976) illustrates both (b) and (c).

(d) There may be other special factors to be considered, as in the *American Cyanamid* case itself, where an interlocutory injunction was granted to prevent infringement of a patent for a pharmaceutical product. The argument was that if the defendant's product had been used prior to the trial, and the claimant then obtained a permanent injunction against its further marketing, the claimant would themselves lose goodwill. Accordingly, the interlocutory injunction prevented the defendants from marketing the product at all.

In *National Commercial Bank Jamaica Ltd* v *Olint Corp Ltd* (2009) the relationship between the award of damages and the grant of an interlocutory injunction was clarified. The Privy Council pointed out that it was often hard to tell whether damages or a cross-undertaking in damages would be an adequate remedy, and the court had to predict whether granting or withholding the injunction was more or less likely to cause irremediable prejudice, and to what extent.

EXAM TIP

You may feel that rather a lot of attention has been given to interlocutory injunctions, but they do appear quite often in exams. In addition, the two special types of injunction set out below are interlocutory.

Freezing order

This is an interlocutory injunction designed to prevent the defendant from disposing of assets which would otherwise be available to meet the claimant's claim, or removing them from the court's jurisdiction. The order is often known as a *Mareva* order from the decision in *Mareva Compania Naviera SA* v *International Bulkcarriers SA* (1980).

The general principles laid down in the *American Cyanamid* case apply to when this remedy will be granted. Also, the claimant should:

■ have a good arguable case;

■ make full and frank disclosure of all material matters together with full particulars of his claim and its amount and should state fairly the points made against it by the defendant;

■ normally give grounds for believing that the defendants have assets in the jurisdiction. All assets are within the scope of a freezing order which has thus been ordered in relation to, for example, bank accounts (the most frequent situation), motor vehicles, jewellery and goodwill;

■ normally give grounds for believing either that the assets will be removed from the jurisdiction before the claim is satisfied, or that in some way they might be dissipated.

See Practice Direction 25A, paragraph 6 for some practice points. This also includes a specimen order which you should study to illustrate an answer on this area.

Search order

This allows search of premises of a possible defendant and is especially useful where a defendant might destroy evidence once a claim form has been served on him. Search orders are used, for example, in cases of alleged video pirating.

In *Anton Piller KG* v *Manufacturing Processes Ltd* (1976), Ormrod LJ laid down the following conditions which must be satisfied by the claimant for the grant of the order:

■ an extremely strong *prima facie* case;

■ actual or potential damage of a very serious nature;

■ clear evidence that the defendant has incriminating documents or things and a real possibility of their destruction before an application without notice can be made.

Make your answer stand out

Search orders were criticised on the ground that they could allow oppressive conduct, amounting to the ransacking of a business, when no case had been proved against the defendant. See Dockray and Laddie (1990) and, for a case example, *Lock International plc* v *Beswick* (1989).

In *Universal Thermosensors* v *Hibben Ltd* (1992) conditions were imposed on the use of these search orders, and these conditions have now been incorporated into the standard form. (The jurisdiction is now statutory: s. 7 Civil Procedure Act 1997 and for the practice see Practice Direction 25A, paragraph 7).

✎ EXAM TIP

Freezing, and especially search orders, is an area where there is room for debate about the need to consider the interests of the party seeking the order and the party against whom it is being sought. Think about this issue for an essay question.

■ Specific performance

✎ EXAM TIP

Exam questions are likely to focus on the circumstances when an order of **specific performance** (SP) may be granted, so look in detail at pairs of slightly contrasting cases and read round them to see whether you can discover any principle. Do not learn masses of cases superficially, but those you learn, learn well!

KEY DEFINITION: Specific performance

This is an order requiring the performance of obligations under a contract. Whereas injunctions are generally negative (i.e. you must not), SP is positive (i.e. you must).

❗ Don't be tempted to . . .

Be careful you don't overlook the distinction between injunctions and specific performance. Some cases appear to deal with injunctions and not SP even though they appear in textbooks under the heading of SP. This is because there is an overlap:

- SP: you must carry out the contract.
- Injunction: you must not fail to carry out the contract.

Therefore, in an exam question on SP you will gain extra marks for bringing in cases involving injunctions which illustrate this overlap.

The fundamental principle is that SP will not normally be granted in certain situations.

Note the use of the word 'normally' in the above sentence. Remember that equity is a discretionary system and so there are fewer black and white rules than in other areas of the law.

- Where damages would be an adequate remedy. The courts ask whether to grant SP would cause hardship or whether it would be impossible to comply with an order of SP.

KEY CASE

Matila Ltd v *Lisheen Properties Ltd* [2010] EWHC 1832 (Ch)

Concerning: principles on which specific performance will be granted

Facts

The purchaser of two apartments had lost its bank funding, partly through the downturn in the property market. Could SP be granted to compel it to complete the purchase?

Legal principle

SP would be granted. The court held that it was only in extraordinary cases that hardship can be a reason not to grant SP. Although inability to perform a contract for financial reasons could raise the defence of impossibility (see *North East Lincolnshire BC* v *Millennium Park (Grimsby) Ltd* (2002)), there was no evidence here that it was impossible to obtain the necessary finance to complete the purchase.

📖 REVISION NOTE

See *Patel* v *Ali* (Chapter 1) for an example of where the defence of hardship did succeed.

 Make your answer stand out

Read Dowling (2011) for a survey on recent cases on SP.

KEY CASE

Sky Petroleum v *VIP Petroleum* **[1974] 1 WLR 576**

Concerning: grant of an injunction, which would amount to specific performance, where damages would not be an adequate remedy

Facts

During a petrol shortage the defendants terminated their contract with the claimants to supply them with petrol.

Legal principle

An injunction was granted restraining the defendants from withholding supplies of petrol. There was a petrol shortage at the time, and if only damages had been awarded to the claimants, they would have been unlikely to obtain supplies elsewhere.

■ Where constant supervision would be needed by the court.

KEY CASE

Co-operative Insurance Society Ltd v *Argyll Stores (Holdings) Ltd* **[1998] AC 1 (HL)**

Concerning: principles to be applied when granting specific performance

Facts

SP was sought of an undertaking to keep a supermarket open during the usual hours of business in a lease which still had 19 years to run. The supermarket was an 'anchor store' in a shopping centre and its closure would badly affect the viability of the rest of the centre.

Legal principle

The House of Lords considered that if the store was ordered to be kept open, the loss to the tenant of the supermarket would exceed that which would be suffered by the landlord if the supermarket closed. In addition, the principle that the court would need to supervise any order of SP remained important.

 Make your answer stand out

This decision was regarded as a setback by those who favour an extension of this remedy (e.g. see Phang (1998)).

■ Where the contract is for personal services.

KEY STATUTE

Trade Union and Labour Relations Act 1992, section 236

This prohibits the courts from enforcing performance of contracts of employment either by specific performance or by injunction. This applies only to actual contracts of employment, not to other contracts of personal service. See *Page One Records* v *Britton (t/a The Troggs)* (1967) and *Warren* v *Mendy* (1989).

KEY CASE

Warner Bros Pictures Inc. v *Nelson* [1937] 1 KB 209 (HC)

Concerning: use of an injunction in contracts of personal service

Facts

The actress (Bette Davis) agreed not to work as an actress for another film company for the period of her contract with Warner Bros.

Legal principle

The injunction would be granted on the ground that Miss Davis could earn a living doing other work. It would not force her to work for Warner Bros.

You should also consider that there have been instances where the courts have enforced a contract for personal services against an employer, i.e. where it has ordered the contract of employment to continue. However, these have been in unusual circumstances as in *Hill* v *CA Parsons and Co. Ltd* (1972).

■ Rescission

KEY DEFINITION: Rescission

This remedy restores the parties to their position before the contract or other transaction was made.

✎ EXAM TIP

You are unlikely to get a detailed question on this but a knowledge of it is useful as it is a common remedy in cases of undue influence.

■ Rectification

KEY DEFINITION: Rectification

Where a written instrument (e.g. a contract) does not accord with the actual intentions of the parties it can be made to do so by an order of rectification.

KEY CASE

Craddock Bros v *Hunt* [1923] 2 Ch 136 (HC)

Concerning: rectification

Facts

A conveyance of a house included the adjacent yard, which actually belonged to another house.

Legal principle

The conveyance would be rectified to exclude the yard.

Note that in *Chartbrook Ltd* v *Persimmon Homes Ltd* (2009) the House of Lords held that, in an action to rectify a document, pre-contractual negotiations were normally inadmissible in construing that contract.

An excellent recent decision for exam purposes, which illustrates both equitable remedies and trust law, is *Kennedy* v *Kennedy* (2014) where the court considered the grant of rescission and rectification where there had been a mistake by trustees (see Chapter 11). This case shows what a mistake it is to pigeonhole your study of equity: instead look for connections between different areas.

Note that by section 50 of the Senior Courts Act 1981 (the modern version of what was known as Lord Cairns Act 1858) the Court of Appeal or High Court may award damages in addition to, or in substitution for, an injunction or specific performance. This should not be confused with what is sometimes called 'equitable compensation' discussed in Chapter 12. Read the recent article by Day (2017).

Equitable doctrines

We will now consider the doctrine of undue influence.

There are other equitable doctrines, but you are less likely to be asked questions on them. Their names, so that you can check whether they are on your syllabus, are:

- Conversion
- Reconversion
- Election
- Performance
- Satisfaction.

Undue influence

Undue influence is a doctrine that, by its nature, is difficult to define precisely but in essence it aims to prevent the vulnerable from exploitation. It is really directed at the manner in which a transaction is entered into.

Example 2.1

A wealthy elderly lady, Florence, has become a recluse and relies for advice on her accountant, Tom, who is the only person she sees regularly apart from her carers. She tells Tom that she intends to make a will but has no one to leave her property to. Tom says that he will give the matter some thought and, in the course of many conversations, gradually persuades her to leave a substantial part of her property to him. A straightforward example of undue influence is *Re Craig* (1971).

KEY CASE

Royal Bank of Scotland v *Etridge (No. 2)* [2001] UKHL 44

Concerning: what is undue influence?

Facts

The facts of this case do not aid an understanding of the legal principle.

Legal principle

Lord Nicholls (HL) held that there is a distinction between:

(a) Cases of actual coercion

(b) Cases where the undue influence arises from a particular relationship.

In (b) there is a subdivision between:

(i) Cases where there is a relationship of trust and confidence between two people. If it is established that there has been a transaction that calls for some explanation, then the burden shifts to the person seeking to uphold the transaction to produce evidence to counter the inference of undue influence.

(ii) Certain types of relationship where one party has acquired influence over another who is vulnerable and dependent, and where substantial gifts by the vulnerable and dependent person are not normally to be expected (e.g. parent and child, trustee and beneficiary, and medical adviser and patient). In these cases, there is a presumption of undue influence by the stronger party over the weaker. *Goodchild* v *Bradbury* (2006) appears to be an example of this category.

The most likely area of undue influence for problem questions is (b) above. It should be noted that (b)(ii) does not include husband and wife, a common scenario for exam problems, and so this situation would fall into (b)(i).

! Don't be tempted to . . .

Make sure that, having first decided that this is a possible undue influence case, you then move on immediately to see where in the above categories it falls. This will decide the rest of the case as it is vital to know whether undue influence has to be proved or not.

Undue influence and third parties

This area has become of great importance in recent years, especially since the decision of the House of Lords in *Barclays Bank plc* v *O'Brien* (1994).

Students often jump straight to this issue when they see it in a problem question and do not ask whether there has been undue influence in the first place. Do this first!

Example 2.2

John persuades Claud, his partner, to enter into a second mortgage of their jointly owned home to the Viper Bank in order to secure some business debts of John. It is clear that John exercised undue influence over Claud to persuade him to sign. The question is whether the Viper Bank is affected by what John has done. If it is not, then although John may be liable to Claud, the actual mortgage is unaffected.

The principles stated by Lord Browne-Wilkinson in *Barclays Bank plc* v *O'Brien* (1994) were the starting point of the law in this case. However, they have been overtaken by those stated by Lord Nicholls in *Etridge* (below) and in a problem question you should concentrate on applying these principles.

Note: In the case below the word 'surety' is used, and here it means the person who has agreed to guarantee the debt, etc. (Claud in the above example).

Royal Bank of Scotland v *Etridge (No. 2)* [2002] 2 AC 773 (HL)

Concerning: (a) when a lender is put on inquiry and (b) steps which a lender should take to avoid being affected by the undue influence of another (e.g. the borrower)

Facts

The facts of this case do not aid an understanding of the legal principle.

Legal principles

These were stated by Lord Nicholls as follows:

(a)   A lender is put on inquiry when one person offers to stand surety for the debts of:
- his or her spouse;
- a person involved in a non-commercial relationship with the surety and the lender is aware of this;
- any company in which any of the above hold shares.

(b)   Steps to be taken when a lender is put on inquiry:
- The lender must contact the surety and request that they nominate a solicitor.
- The surety must reply, nominating a solicitor.
- The lender must, with the consent of the surety, disclose to the solicitor all relevant information – both the debtor's financial position and the details of the proposed loan. (*HSBC Bank* v *Brown* (2015) emphasised that the bank must furnish the nominated solicitor with information that would enable the solicitor to explain the financial risks to be assumed by the surety.)
- The solicitor must advise the surety in a face-to-face meeting at which the debtor is not present. The advice must cover an explanation of the documentation and the risks to the surety in signing, and emphasise that the surety must decide whether to proceed.
- The solicitor must, if satisfied that the surety wishes to proceed, send written confirmation to the lender that the solicitor has explained the nature of the documents and their implications to the surety.

 Make your answer stand out

The principle in *O'Brien* and the decision in *Etridge* (above) have been the subject of a great deal of academic debate. A good place to start is the article by Andrews (2002).

Consequences of undue influence

If the transaction is affected by undue influence, then it is voidable.

! **Don't be tempted to . . .**

Be sure you consider the *extent* to which the mortgage is set aside:

- *TSB Bank plc* v *Camfield* (1995): the whole mortgage was set aside.
- *Dunbar Bank plc* v *Nadeem* (1997): it was set aside only on condition that the claimant accounted to the mortgagee for the benefit she had from it.

Misrepresentation and undue influence

Instead of, or in addition to, the possibility of undue influence, an exam question may ask you whether there has been **misrepresentation**. You will probably not need to remember as much on this as you did in your contract days, but do note the definition.

KEY DEFINITION: Misrepresentation

This is an untrue statement of fact that induces a person to enter into a transaction.

Look out for where undue influence and misrepresentation are possibly combined, i.e. X uses undue influence to persuade Y, his partner, to sign a mortgage but also lies about, for example, how much the mortgage is for.

 Make your answer stand out

Read 'Mortgages and undue influence' (Thompson, 2003). It provides an excellent critical study of the law.

▇ Putting it all together

Answer guidelines

See the essay question at the start of this chapter.

Approaching the question

This is a very typical question in equity exams and requires you to think about the nature of equitable remedies. What you must *not* do is to just plough through the remedies summarising them.

Important points to include

Start with an introduction that addresses the issue: what is meant by discretionary? Look back to *Patel* v *Ali* and discuss how the word 'discretionary' was applied. The essential point is that, although there are no rigid rules about when equitable remedies will be granted or refused, there are principles.

Now go on to select cases illustrating principles in the grant of equitable remedies – look back through the material in this chapter and select cases that you think you can use and research them. Try to include recent cases, e.g. *Matila Ltd* v *Lisheen Properties Ltd* (2010) and contrast cases showing different approaches.

 Make your answer stand out

Range beyond the equitable remedies dealt with in this chapter. Go to Chapter 8 on constructive trusts and refer to the remedial constructive trust. This is said to be a remedy. Is it? If it is, it is certainly discretionary, but what are the principles that govern its exercise? Are there any?

Note also that in the dishonest assistance case of *Novoship (UK) Ltd* v *Nikitin* (2014) the remedy of an account of profits was emphasised to be discretionary.

READ TO IMPRESS

Andrews, G. (2002) Undue influence – where's the disadvantage? 66 *Conv.* 456.

Day, W. (2017) Restitution for wrongs: one step in the right direction? 133 *LQR* 384

Dockray, M. and Laddie, H. (1990) Piller problems. 106 *LQR* 661.

Dowling, A. (2011) Vendors' application for specific performance. 3 *Conv.* 208.

Phang, A. (1998) Specific performance – explaining the roots of settled practice. 61 *MLR* 421.

Thompson, M. (2003) Mortgages and undue influence, in Cooke, E. (ed.) *Modern Studies in Property Law,* 2nd edn. Oxford: Hart Publishing.

www.pearsoned.co.uk/lawexpress

Go online to access more revision support including quizzes to test your knowledge, sample questions with answer guidelines, printable versions of the topic maps, and more!

The three certainties

3

■ Topic map

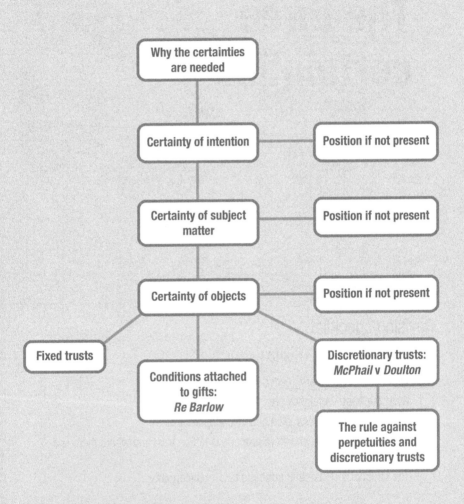

■ Introduction

This topic often appears in exam questions. Questions often contain a number of issues covering all the three certainties, so this is a good topic on which you can pick up those extra marks.

Three certainties questions usually involve clauses in wills, although certainties issues can arise in *inter vivos* gifts also.

There are two reasons for requiring certainty in the creation of a trust:

1. A practical one. It would be wrong for the court to impose a trust where none was intended. Trusteeship can be an onerous task and so no one should be held liable as a trustee unless this was clearly intended.

2. The need for the court to be able to control the trust (*Morice* v *Bishop of Durham* (1805)).

ASSESSMENT ADVICE

Essay questions

Essay questions are likely to deal with any of the areas dealt with in this chapter, all of which have led to a great deal of academic debate:

- ■ Certainty of subject matter where the goods are not yet ascertained, as in *Re London Wine Co.* (1986).

- ■ The tests for certainty of objects, especially in discretionary trusts, but also possibly in fixed trusts and where there is a condition precedent.

- ■ The decisions in *McPhail* v *Doulton* (1971) and *Re Barlow's Will Trusts* (1979) are worth looking at in detail. Make sure that you understand the debates surrounding them.

Problem questions

The three certainties is one of the favourite areas for problem questions. It is not difficult to gain a reasonable pass on them, but if you are looking for a really good mark you need to go deeper than just running through the requirements of certainty and concentrate on discussing any problematic areas such as those mentioned in the essay question advice above. You can also boost your mark when answering problem questions by paying very close attention to the actual words used in the creation of a trust and analysing them carefully. To sum up: this is a good area in which you can aim to score highly.

■ Sample question

Could you answer this question? Below is a typical problem question that could arise on this topic. An outline answer is included at the end of the chapter, while a sample essay question and guidance on tackling it can be found on the companion website.

PROBLEM QUESTION

Susan, who died recently, left a will containing the following bequests:

1. £250,000 to my husband, John, safe in the knowledge that he will provide for our children.

2. £10,000 to my daughter, Barbara, provided that she allows my sister, Eileen, a reasonable sum each year to provide her with a few of the little comforts of life.

3. My collection of rare books shall be available for any friend of mine who wishes to select a book in memory of me.

4. £300,000 to be distributed, at the discretion of my trustees, among employees, ex-employees, their friends and relations of my late husband's company, Midland Optical Illusion Ltd.

Can you advise Arthur, Susan's executor, on the validity of these gifts?

■ What are the three certainties?

These are:

- ■ certainty of intention to create a trust;
- ■ certainty of the subject matter of the trust;
- ■ certainty of the objects of the trust.

These requirements have been set out in many cases – for example, by Lord Langdale in *Knight* v *Knight* (1840).

Certainty of intention

Certainty of intention means that the person who is given the property shall hold it on trust, i.e. it is evidence that the settlor or testator intended to impose a binding obligation that the property was to be held on trust. Often common sense and an ability to see clearly what precise words and phrases mean is enough when answering a problem question.

Example 3.1

(a) John by will leaves £1,000 to Albert and says that he would like Albert to look after his children.

(b) John leaves £1,000 to Albert on trust for his children.

It is obvious that (b) is a trust but that (a) is not. Why? Because in (a) there is only a request. It is often said that 'precatory words do not create a trust'. Precatory words are words such as 'request', 'hope' and 'desire' which do not impose a trust and where the recipient can keep the property as a gift. A good example is *Re Diggles* (1888), where the word 'desire' did not create a trust.

✎ EXAM TIP

■ Use your common sense – do the words used look like the imposition of a trust?

■ Look at all the words used – not just particular ones.

Compare the following cases.

KEY CASE

Re Adams and Kensington Vestry (1884) 27 Ch D 394 (CA)

Concerning: certainty of intention

Facts

The testator gave his estate to his wife 'in full confidence that she will do what is right as to the disposal thereof between my children . . . '.

Legal principle

The words 'in full confidence' did not create a trust.

KEY CASE

Comiskey v *Bowring-Hanbury* [1905] AC 84 (HL)

Concerning: certainty of intention

Facts

A testator gave his property to his wife 'in full confidence that at her death she will devise it to one or more of my nieces as she shall think fit'. If she did not do this then the will directed that the property should be divided equally among the nieces. It was held that this created a trust.

▶

> **Legal principle**
>
> Look at the meaning of the words used taken as a whole and not in isolation. Although the words 'in full confidence' were used here as in *Adams* (above), the second sentence here was clearly mandatory and so created a trust.

KEY CASE

> *Vucicevic* v *Aleksic* [2017] EWHC 2335 (Ch)
>
> *Concerning: certainty of intention to create a trust*
>
> **Facts**
>
> The testator made a handwritten will leaving the Serbian Orthodox Church three houses and 'all the money that was left after taxes' for people in need in Kosovo, especially children. He placed a senior bishop of the Church in charge of the gift, expressing 'full confidence' that he would ensure that the benefit went to the right place. Did these words create a trust?
>
> **Legal principle**
>
> The court held that they did. Although the words 'in full confidence' were problematic the gift had to be looked at in context: the testator had no wife, partner or children and the gift was to the Church for charitable purposes. The confidence was placed in the bishop as a person in a position of authority whom he trusted to make the right decisions.

Another recent instance is *Day v Harris* (2013) where the words 'to share and keep or sell if you like' on a note posted at the same time as boxes were handed over, indicated a gift to the recipients and not a trust for the donor's carer, to whom he had left most of his property by will.

 Make your answer stand out

Learn some more examples of equity in this area (e.g. *R v Clowes (No. 2)* (1994)). This also illustrates a link between equity and the law of theft: you can impress the examiner with your knowledge of this!

See *Re Farepak Food and Gifts Ltd (in administration)* (2006) in Chapter 7. This is an excellent case for essay questions as it contains material on express, resulting and constructive trusts.

The *effect* of the lack of certainty of intention is that the donee (no trustee here) takes the property as an absolute gift.

Certainty of subject matter

This is simple enough: there is no point in creating a trust by showing certainty of intention if we do not know what property is to be held on trust.

KEY CASE

Anthony v *Donges* [1998] 2 FLR 775 (HC)

Concerning: certainty of subject matter

Facts

A widow was left 'such minimal part of the estate as she might be entitled to . . . for maintenance purposes'.

Legal principle

There was no certainty of subject matter.

See also *Palmer* v *Simmonds* (1854): 'the bulk of my estate' was too uncertain.

KEY CASE

Re Golay [1965] 1 WLR 969

Concerning: apparent lack of certainty of subject matter

Facts

Executors under a will were directed to allow a beneficiary 'to enjoy the use of one of my flats and receive a reasonable income from my other properties'.

Legal principle

Although the word 'reasonable' seemed too uncertain, the gift was upheld as the court assumed that it referred to the beneficiary's previous standard of living.

KEY CASE

Curtis v *Rippon* (1820) 5 Madd 434 (HC)

Concerning: the possibility that a person is intended to be a trustee of part but to receive the other part as a gift

Facts

A widow received all her husband's property subject to a trust where she was to 'use the property for her spiritual and temporal good and that of the children, remembering always according to circumstances the Church of God and the poor'. It was held that as the ▶

shares to be taken by the children, the Church and the poor were uncertain, the widow took all as there was no doubt that she was intended to benefit to some extent.

Legal principle

Where the shares to be taken by the beneficiaries are uncertain but there is also an absolute gift (often to the intended trustee), then the gift takes effect.

Students sometimes say at this point: 'But it is a fundamental principle that a trustee cannot benefit from the trust.' This is quite right. But the point is that there is no trust as there is no certainty of subject matter.

KEY CASE

Re London Wine Co. (Shippers) Ltd [1986] PCC 121 (HC)

Concerning: certainty of subject matter where goods are unascertained

Facts

Buyers of wine which was stored at a warehouse claimed that it was held on trust for them, but the claim failed as the wine had not been separated from a larger stock of similar wine held at the warehouse.

Legal principle

Trust property must be ascertainable.

 Make your answer stand out

Look also, for example, at *Hunter* v *Moss* (1994) and *Re Goldcorp Exchange Ltd (in receivership)* (1995). Read the criticism of *Hunter* v *Moss* by Hayton (1994).

The *effect* of the lack of certainty of subject matter is:

■ if there is no certainty of what the subject matter is, then there can be no trust as there is nothing to hold on trust;

■ if the attempted trust has been attached to a gift, then the gift becomes absolute as in *Curtis* v *Rippon* (1820) (above).

Certainty of objects (i.e. beneficiaries)

Note at the outset that the rules differ depending on the type of trust (see Figure 3.1).

Figure 3.1

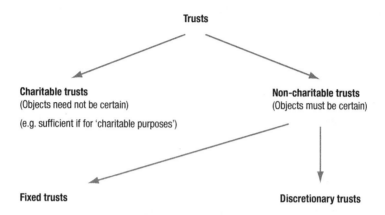

This chapter will deal with non-charitable trusts (private trusts) as one exam question would be unlikely to deal with certainties in both charitable and non-charitable trusts.

Check Chapter 9 for certainty of objects in charitable trusts.

It is vital that you recognise and can apply the distinction between fixed and discretionary trusts.

■ Fixed trusts

KEY DEFINITION: Fixed trust

Where the interests in the trust property are fixed in the trust instrument.

Example 3.2

'To all my children in equal shares.'

Here there is no room for any discretion by the trustees.

KEY DEFINITION: Rule for certainty of objects in fixed trusts

All the beneficiaries must be capable of being listed, i.e. there must be no doubt as to who the beneficiaries are: *IRC* v *Broadway Cottages Trust* (1955).

This is really common sense when applied to the above example. Each child is to have an equal amount and so the division cannot be made until we know how many to divide the sum by.

▉ Discretionary trusts

KEY DEFINITION: Discretionary trust

Where the trustees have a discretion as to whether a person will be a beneficiary or not.

KEY CASE

McPhail v *Doulton* **[1971] AC 424 (HL)**

Concerning: certainty of objects in discretionary trusts

Facts

A trust provided that the trustees were to apply the income from a fund at their absolute discretion for the benefit of any officers and employees of a (named) company together with ex-officers and ex-employees and their relatives and dependants. This was sufficiently certain.

Legal principle

In discretionary trusts the test for certainty of objects was laid down by Lord Wilberforce and is known as the 'individual ascertainability test'.

KEY DEFINITION: Rule for certainty of objects in discretionary trusts

Can it be said with certainty that any given individual is or is not a member of the class?

As you can see from the facts, it would be impossible to list all the beneficiaries (e.g. who are the relatives?). However, it must be possible to say with certainty whether a particular person is a beneficiary.

Example 3.3

A gift to my old mates. This does not satisfy the test of certainty as it is not possible to say with certainty whether anyone is an old mate.

Example 3.4

A gift to my cousins. This does satisfy the test, as it is possible to say with certainty whether a person is a cousin.

Make your answer stand out

Look at the judgments in the HC and CA in *Re Baden's Deed Trusts (No. 2)* (1973) where the test laid down by the HL in *McPhail* v *Doulton* was applied.

Conceptual and evidential uncertainty

Re Baden's Deed Trusts (No. 2) (1973) distinguished between conceptual and evidential uncertainty. Example 3.3 is a case of conceptual uncertainty in that the whole concept of a mate is not capable of precise definition and so the gift will fail. Example 3.4 is an example of evidential uncertainty in that it may be difficult to establish who is a cousin, but that is no bar to a person coming forward and proving that he or she *is* a cousin.

Effect of a lack of certainty

Provided that the other two certainties are present, the property will be held on a resulting trust for the settlor or, if the trust is created by will, then for the testator's estate or, if the testator was intestate, for those entitled on intestacy.

Note these other points in certainty of objects in discretionary trusts:

- *Trustees have a duty to appreciate the 'width of the field'* (Megarry VC in *Re Hay's Settlement Trusts* (1982)). This means that although they cannot draw up a complete list of the objects, they should not distribute the property until they have decided whether the selection is to be made 'merely from a dozen or instead, thousands or millions'.
- There is some authority for saying that the trust will not be enforced if the width of objects makes it 'administratively unworkable'. In *R* v *District Auditor, ex parte West Yorkshire MCC* (1986), a trust for the inhabitants of West Yorkshire (about 2.5 million people) failed on this ground.

Power to cure uncertainty

This can arise in two situations:

(a) Where there is uncertainty about a particular *fact*. A third party can be made a judge of this.

Re Tuck's Settlement Trusts [1978] Ch 49 (HC)

Concerning: decision on whether a person satisfies the criteria to be made by a third party

Facts

A chief rabbi was made judge of whether a person was of Jewish blood.

Legal principle

This was valid as the decision was to be based on measurable criteria.

(b)   Where there is conceptual uncertainty.

Example 3.5

John's will provides that each of his old drinking pals at the Black Bush shall have a bottle of whisky and that, in case of doubt, the landlord of the Black Bush shall have the power to decide who they are.

Given that the phrase 'old drinking pals at the Black Bush' is conceptually uncertain, does the power given to the landlord save it?

The probability is that this would not save the gift as the phrase 'old drinking pals at the Black Bush' is conceptually uncertain and so a power to decide is irrelevant: what can the landlord decide? In addition, the court cannot control the trust (e.g. see *Re Jones* (1953)).

Conditions precedent and certainty of objects

Re Barlow's Will Trusts [1979] 1 WLR 278 (HC)

Concerning: certainty of objects where there is a condition precedent

Facts

A will directed that a friend of the testator should be allowed to purchase any of her paintings. The court held that a friend was a person who had met the testator frequently when circumstances allowed on a social and not a business occasion. On this basis the gift was allowed to stand.

Legal principle

Gifts subject to conditions precedent are subject to a less strict test than those in discretionary trusts as the amount that one person receives does not affect what others will receive.

 Make your answer stand out

This case is controversial and you should be prepared to discuss whether it is correct. See Emery (1982) for an excellent article that goes to the heart of the issues.

✎ **EXAM TIP**

Students often apply the test in *Re Barlow's Will Trusts* (1979) whenever they see the word 'friend' in a question. This may be wrong. If £100 is left to be shared on a discretionary trust 'among all my friends', this would fail as the test in *McPhail* v *Doulton* (1971) would apply and 'friends' would not satisfy it.

■ The rule against perpetuities and discretionary trusts

There are two perpetuity rules: one against remoteness of vesting affects discretionary trusts; the other is concerned with purpose trusts and is dealt with in Chapter 10.

Effect of the rule against remoteness of vesting

Example 3.6

John leaves £1,000 to Gilbert to hold for 'the benefit of all my employees and ex-employees, their families and dependants'. Assuming that this is valid (see *McPhail* v *Doulton* (above)), we must decide when the trust is to end.

KEY DEFINITION: Rule against remoteness of vesting

Section 5 of the Perpetuities and Accumulations Act 2009 provides for a period of 125 years, which overrides any different provision in the trust instrument. However, section 16 of this Act inserts a new section 5A into the Perpetuities and Accumulations Act 1964 which provides that the new period will not apply to a will executed before the 2009 Act came into force on 6 April 2010. Here the former rule will apply, which provided that a period of 80 years could be specified.

It is most unlikely that you will get a detailed question on the notoriously complex subject of perpetuities, but it will certainly boost your marks if you mention it.

■ Putting it all together

Answer guidelines

See the problem question at the start of this chapter.

Approaching the question

Note carefully exactly what the question asks you to do. Here it asks you to advise on the validity of the gifts. If the gifts are not valid trusts, then who gets the property? Always find a home for the property! Make it a habit to check at the end of answering a certainties question (and other trusts questions) that you have decided where the property will go.

Deal with all three certainties when looking at each situation, even if in some cases the answer is so obvious that you need not spend much time on some areas.

Never waste time in dealing with the question of the validity of the will. Do not set out the formalities for a valid will unless the question asks you to do this. Assume that the will is valid and go straight to the certainties issues unless directed otherwise. It would be very unlikely that some issue of the validity of the will would arise in a question like this.

Important points to include

Part (a). 'Safe in the knowledge': this may not satisfy the requirement of certainty of intention. Look at the cases (e.g. *Re Adams and Kensington Vestry*) and decide whether it indicates the imposition of a trust. If there is no trust, there will be an absolute gift to John.

Part (b). There is probably certainty of intention: 'provided that', although this should be discussed. The problem is that there appears to be no certainty of subject matter unless the principle in *Re Golay* applies and external evidence can establish what a reasonable sum is – the words 'a few of the little comforts of life' may help here. If there is no trust, then the whole sum will go to Barbara.

Part (c). Can the *Re Barlow* principle apply? This seems to be a conditional gift, as being a friend is a condition of selecting a book. If so, then provided that the court is prepared to lay down conditions for friendship, the gift will be valid.

Part (d). There is no doubt of certainty of intention and subject matter (but gain a few marks by just pointing this out), but is there certainty of objects? A close look at *McPhail* v *Doulton* is needed here, as this is a discretionary trust. Mention and apply the distinction between evidential and conceptual uncertainty. It is probably valid. If not, a resulting trust for Susan's estate.

 Make your answer stand out

Apply *Vucicevic* v *Aleksic* [2017] to the certainty of intention issue in (a) and (b). Analyse the situation in (c) carefully and explain clearly the decision in *Re Barlow* and any problems associated with it.

READ TO IMPRESS

Emery, C. (1982) The most hallowed principle. 98 *LQR* 551.

Harris, J. (1971) Trust, power and duty. 87 *LQR* 31.

Hayton, D. (1994) Uncertainty of subject matter of trusts. 110 *LQR* 335.

www.pearsoned.co.uk/lawexpress

 Go online to access more revision support including quizzes to test your knowledge, sample questions with answer guidelines, printable versions of the topic maps, and more!

Formalities

4

Topic map

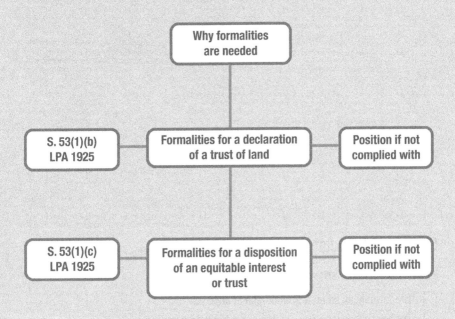

■ Introduction

The basic principles of formalities are reasonably straightforward and the number of variations on them is not great.

A good attempt at a problem on formalities will be well rewarded. In addition, the subject provides excellent material for essay questions.

Remember also that, in order to be valid, a trust must not only comply with any requisite formalities, it must also comply with the three certainties. Check Chapter 3 and make sure that you can recall the three certainties.

ASSESSMENT ADVICE

Essay questions

Essays in this area will require you to have read and mastered the essential detail of the complex cases such as *Oughtred* v *IRC* (1960) and *Vandervell* v *IRC* (1967), and have looked at the justification for these rules. You may also have a question on other issues such as the constitution of a trust where you will need to deal with this area.

Problem questions

These will usually deal with a variety of situations and ask you whether the statutory provisions on the formalities will apply and, if so, what the effect of non-observance will be. Draw a diagram of the situations and remember that these types of problem question are asking you for a sound, logical approach. Spend time before writing to get your ideas in order.

■ Sample question

Could you answer this question? Below is a typical problem question that could arise on this topic. Guidelines on answering the question are included at the end of this chapter, while a sample essay question and guidance on tackling it can be found on the companion website.

PROBLEM QUESTION

Isabel owns a house, The Gables, and also has £20,000 in an account at the Worcester Bank. In addition she is the beneficiary under a trust fund, consisting of 1,000 shares in ABC Co. Ltd, set up for her by her late father, Albert, of which her brother, Frank, is now the trustee. She says to her son, Larry, 'In future I will hold The Gables for you but it will still stay in my name. The same applies to the money in the Worcester Bank.' She then rings Frank and says, 'I really do not need those shares in the ABC Co. any more. In future pay any dividends to Larry.'

The next day Isabel dies and Hubert, her **executor**, asks your advice on whether and to what extent The Gables, the £20,000 in the bank account and the shares in the ABC Co. Ltd form part of Isabel's estate.

Declaration of a trust of land

Law of Property Act 1925, section 53(1)(b)

'A declaration of trust concerning land or any interest therein must be manifested and proved by some writing signed by some person who is able to declare the same or by his will.'

Example 4.1

Claud is the owner of a house known as 'The Laurels' and says to some friends, 'From now on I am holding "The Laurels" in trust for my children Tom and Tim.' This is not enforceable, as there is nothing in writing.

Points to note:

- The actual declaration of trust need not be in writing. The words 'manifested and proved' require only written evidence of the details of the trust and do not require that the actual trust should be in writing. Therefore evidence can be, for example, in two or more documents which are linked.
- The signature of the settlor is probably needed. The words in section 53(1)(b) are 'signed by some person who is able to declare the same' and this is generally taken to mean that an agent cannot sign, although the point has never been decided.
- The requirement in section 53(1)(b) applies only to express trusts and not to resulting, implied or constructive trusts (s. 53(2)). This exception is of great importance as it has

enabled the courts to impose a resulting, implied or constructive trust in many cases where there was no written declaration of trust. See Chapter 8 of this book and Chapter 4 of the companion book *Land Law* in the Law Express series.

■ No formalities are required for *inter vivos* declarations of trusts of other property. Where the trust is created by will there are statutory requirements but these will not be relevant for an exam on trusts as wills fall within the law of succession.

📖 REVISION NOTE

Good examples of section 53(2) are those involving disputes over the beneficial entitlement to the family home and where it is felt necessary to impose a trust to prevent fraud or unconscionable conduct (see Chapter 8 and below).

Note the distinction between the formalities requirements and constitution of a trust (Chapter 5). Constitution deals with the actual transfer of the trust property, but here we are concerned with a preliminary issue: did the actual declaration of a trust observe the required formalities?

Failure to observe the requirements of section 53(1)(b)

Section 53(1)(b) is silent on the position when these requirements are not complied with, but it is accepted that this will not make the trust void but only unenforceable (*Gardner* v *Rowe* (1828)). *Void* means that the trust is of no effect at all. *Unenforceable* means that, although the trust is valid, it cannot be enforced in any legal proceedings.

However, in the case below, the court held that a trust could be imposed where the effect of the operation of section 53(1)(b) would be to permit fraud.

KEY CASE

Rochefoucauld v *Boustead* [1897] 1 Ch 196 (CA)

Concerning: whether a formality requirement should be set aside as it is an instrument of fraud

Facts

The claimant had mortgaged land but was having difficulty in repaying the mortgage. The defendant bought the land and orally agreed to hold it as trustee for the claimant. However, he treated the land as his own.

Legal principle

The claimant was entitled to an account of profits made on the land. The trust was not in writing and so did not satisfy the requirements of what is now section 53(1)(b), LPA 1925 and was thus technically unenforceable. However, it would be a fraud on the defendant's part to shelter behind section 53(1)(b) and take the profits for himself. Therefore a trust would be enforced.

Make your answer stand out

This case is sometimes used as an example of the operation of constructive trusts as the 'instrument of fraud' principle is usually found in that context. You will gain marks for pointing out that here an express trust was apparently imposed, but you should also point out that in other cases the courts have thought that a resulting or a constructive trust was more appropriate and, of course, these trusts are exempted from the formality requirement of section 53(1)(b) by section 53(2) above. An instance of this is *Hodgson* v *Marks* (1971) (see Chapter 7).

There is also a debate on whether the trust here was express or constructive and this is linked to another debate on whether section 53(1)(b) provides for a rule of enforceability or one of evidence. You can really boost your marks by looking at this – see Swadling (2009) and then Liew (2012).

■ Dispositions of equitable interests arising under trusts

It is vital to be absolutely clear about when this happens by contrast with a declaration of trust, which was dealt with above. One simple way is this:

- Section 53(1)(b) applies when a trust is being declared.
- Section 53(1)(c) applies when the trust is in force, but it is intended to move the interests of beneficiaries under it (i.e. equitable interests) from one person to another.

Note that these two subsections operate at different stages (see Figure 4.1).

Do not assume that all the cases in this area are tax cases: *Drakeford* v *Cotton* (2012) concerned ownership of a joint bank account.

KEY STATUTE

Law of Property Act 1925, section 53(1)(c)

A disposition of an equitable interest or trust must be in writing and signed either by the settlor or by his/her authorised agent.

Points to note:

- The actual disposition must be in writing. Written evidence will not suffice.
- The signature of an agent is sufficient.
- Section 53(1)(c) does not, by virtue of section 53(2), apply to resulting, implied or constructive trusts.

Figure 4.1

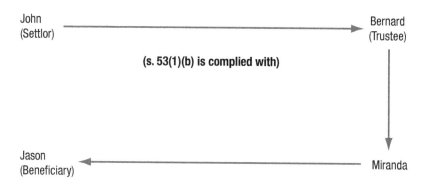

John declares in writing that his house 'Equity' is now held by Bernard in trust for Miranda

John
(Settlor) → Bernard
(Trustee)

(s. 53(1)(b) is complied with)

Jason
(Beneficiary) ← Miranda

Miranda by writing transfers her interest in 'Equity' to Jason

(s. 53(1)(c) is complied with)

- Where a disposition of an equitable interest is made which is to be held on trust, then although the actual disposition must be in writing, the details of the trust need not be (*Re Tyler's Fund Trusts* (1967)).

- There is no requirement for the trustees to be notified of the disposition. (This is a useful point to add in an exam answer.)

> ✎ **EXAM TIP**
>
> Do not go into too much detail on the facts of cases in this area: it is the basic principles they illustrate that matter. This is not a tax law exam!

Application of section 53(1)(c)

An exam question will deal with situations where the application of section 53(1)(c) has been considered by the courts. We will now look at each of these but, before we do, you may find the following quote from Garton (2015: 152) useful: 'If at the commencement of a transaction a person has a subsisting equitable interest and at the end no longer has that interest, then there has been a disposition within section 53(1)(c).'

The reason why many of the cases discussed in this chapter were brought was that settlors have tried to avoid payment of stamp duty, which is payable on the written instrument by which property is transferred; but many settlors have argued that, as a particular transaction is not a disposition within the meaning of section 53(1)(c), no writing is needed and therefore payment of stamp duty is not required.

In the following examples, T holds on trust for X absolutely. T is the trustee and X is the beneficiary.

Transfer by beneficiary (X) of her equitable interest to another

In Figure 4.2 writing is obviously needed.

Figure 4.2

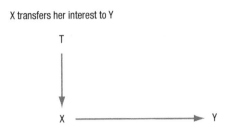

X transfers her interest to Y

Direction by a beneficiary (X) to trustees that they are now to hold on trust for another person

Figure 4.3 shows an example.

Figure 4.3

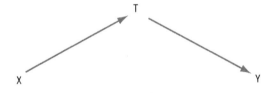

X directs T to hold the property on trust for Y

KEY CASE

Grey v *IRC* [1960] AC 1 (HL)

Concerning: whether a direction by a beneficiary to trustees to hold the trust property on trust for another is a disposition within section 53(1)(c)

Facts

The settlor transferred shares to trustees to hold as nominees for him. He then orally (i.e. no writing) directed the trustees to hold the shares on trust for his grandchildren and the trustees later executed a written declaration of trust.

Legal principle

A direction by a beneficiary to trustees to hold on trust for another is a disposition within section 53(1)(c).

Transfer of the legal estate by a bare trustee to another

KEY DEFINITION: Bare trustee

A bare trustee is a trustee with no active duties and so can be given directions by the beneficiary to transfer the legal estate.

Example 4.2

X (beneficiary) directs T to transfer shares to Y so that Y becomes the absolute owner. A possible form of words could be: 'All my interest in the shares is to go to Y.' The word 'all' could mean that not only the equitable interest in the shares (which belongs to X) but also the legal title to them (which is held by T) should go to Y.

KEY CASE

Vandervell v *IRC* [1967] 2 AC 291 (HL)

Concerning: whether a transfer of the legal estate, where there is an existing equitable interest, to another requires writing under section 53(1)(c)

Facts

A bank which held shares for Vandervell as a **bare trustee** transferred them, on his directions, to the Royal College of Surgeons subject to an option exercisable by Vandervell Trustees Ltd to repurchase the shares. The bank's legal title to the shares and Vandervell's equitable interest in them were accordingly both transferred and it was held that this transaction was not caught by section 53(1)(c) and so writing was not needed.

Legal principle

A direction to transfer the legal estate to another does not require writing.

Although the equitable interest passes from X to Y this is done automatically with the transfer of the legal estate and thus there is no separate disposition.

New trusts are declared by the trustee with the consent of the beneficiary

Example 4.3

T declares, with the agreement of X, that he now holds the property on trust for W.

KEY CASE

Re Vandervell's Trusts (No. 2) [1974] Ch 269 (CA)

Concerning: declaration of new trusts

Facts

Following from the decision in *Vandervell* v *IRC* (above), Vandervell instructed Vandervell Trustees to exercise the option to repurchase the shares which were then intended to be held on the trusts of the Vandervell children's settlement.

Legal principle

It was held that where new trusts were declared with the consent of the beneficiary then, as this was not within section 53(1)(c), writing was not required.

 Make your answer stand out

Consider why there was a different decision in *Grey* v *IRC* (above) from that in *Re Vandervell's Trusts*. In both there was a direction to trustees but in *Grey*, section 53 (1)(c) applied whereas in *Vandervell* it did not. Is one explanation that in *Vandervell* there was initially a resulting trust of the shares for Vandervell which ceased to exist when the shares were repurchased? Is this a valid distinction?

Beneficiary contracts to transfer his equitable interest

Example 4.4

X contracts with Y to transfer X's interest in the trust to Y.

The law here awaits clarification and the leading case is:

KEY CASE

Oughtred v *IRC* [1960] AC 206 (HL)

Concerning: whether a contract to transfer a beneficial interest under a trust is caught by section 53(1)(c)

Facts

X and Y had separate interests in shares in a private company. They orally agreed to exchange their interests and the IRC claimed stamp duty on the actual written transfer of the shares.

Legal principle

In the case of a contract to sell shares in a private company, the remedy of specific performance is available because the shares are unique and so a constructive trust arises in favour of the buyer. However, the buyer does not acquire a full beneficial interest until the formal written transfer. This is therefore the disposition and section 53(1)(c) applies to it. Lord Radcliffe, however, dissented and held that Mrs Oughtred obtained the ownership in equity by virtue of the oral agreement.

 Make your answer stand out

Neville v *Wilson* (1997) supports Lord Radcliffe's argument (see Figure 4.4). See Milne (1997). However, in *Parinv* v *IRC* (1998) the majority decision in *Oughtred* was followed. Something may depend on whether it is a tax case. *Neville* v *Wilson* was not; *Parinv (Hatfield) Ltd* v *IRC* was. Neville v Wilson was followed in *Singh* v *Anand* (2007).

Figure 4.4

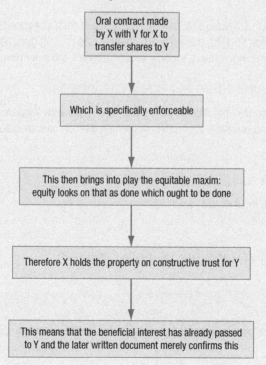

The sequence of events in the example based on Lord Radcliffe's dissent in *Oughtred* v *IRC* is:

Oral contract made by X with Y for X to transfer shares to Y

↓

Which is specifically enforceable

↓

This then brings into play the equitable maxim: equity looks on that as done which ought to be done

↓

Therefore X holds the property on constructive trust for Y

↓

This means that the beneficial interest has already passed to Y and the later written document merely confirms this

Beneficiary declares herself trustee

As a sub-trust has been created (Figure 4.5), it can be argued that this is a declaration of trust and so it falls within section 53(1)(b), in which case writing is needed only if it concerns land. However, if X has no active duties to perform and is thus a bare trustee, is the effect that X will have disappeared from the picture and there may be a disposition from X to Y?

Figure 4.5

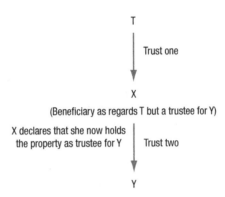

In *Nelson* v *Greening & Sykes (Builders) Ltd* (2007) it was held, in a case not involving the application of section 53(1)(c), that an intermediate trustee (i.e. X) does not necessarily cease to be a trustee. However, as regards section 53(1)(c), the point remains open.

Beneficiary surrenders her equitable interest

The position is uncertain, but it could be argued, by analogy with *Vandervell* v *IRC* (above), that as the legal and equitable titles are now merged there is no disposition.

Example 4.5

X surrenders her interest to T1 and T2.

Beneficiary disclaims her equitable interest

Example 4.6

X, as soon as she becomes aware that she has an equitable interest, disclaims it.

KEY CASE

Re Paradise Motor Co. Ltd [1968] 1 WLR 1125 (HC)

Concerning: disclaimer of an equitable interest

Facts

The facts were the same as in the example.

Legal principle

Writing is not needed here because 'a disclaimer operates by way of avoidance and not by way of disposition' (Danckwerts LJ).

See also Glister, J. (2014), discussed also in Chapter 6, for another angle on the position where there is a disclaimer.

Beneficiary under a staff pension fund appoints a nominee to receive benefits from the fund

Example 4.7

X, a beneficiary under a staff pension fund, appoints T to receive the money payable by the fund in the event of X's death.

KEY CASE

Re Danish Bacon Co. Ltd Staff Pension Fund [1971] 1 WLR 248 (HC)

Concerning: nominations of benefits in a pension fund

Facts

An employee had nominated his wife to receive benefits payable to him under a pension fund and had then, by a separate letter, changed his mind.

Legal principle

Megarry J doubted whether this was a disposition requiring writing, but, if it was, the writing was supplied by connecting the two documents.

📖 REVISION NOTE

See *Zeital* v *Kaye* (2010) in Chapter 5 for a significant case in which the requirements of section 53(1)(c) were applied.

Failure to comply with the requirements of section 53(1)(c)

The result is that the disposition is void.

Why formalities are needed

■ To prevent fraud.

Example 4.8

John says that Susan has declared that she now holds her house on trust for him. Susan denies this. The only way in which John can prove this is by producing written evidence. This is the same principle as the requirement of writing in an actual contract for the sale of land.

■ To enable the trustees to know what is going on.

Example 4.9

Gerald is a trustee of property for Jane. Jane tells Gerald that she has transferred her interest to Mark and in future Gerald should treat Mark as the beneficiary. What if Jane is wrong? Gerald must require writing to prove that Jane's beneficial interest has been transferred to Mark.

 Make your answer stand out

The complexity of this area has led to calls for reform. The Law Commission proposed to issue a Consultation Paper in 1999 which could have led to legislation but, due to work on other projects it was put back and there is no date for any proposals. Look at Battersby (1979) for a critique of the law.

■ Putting it all together

Answer guidelines

See the problem question at the start of this chapter.

Approaching the question

Begin by explaining why Hubert's question is important. If Isabel has really divested herself of any interest in the property, then it will no longer form part of her estate. Then look at each point in turn.

Important points to include

The Gables: this appears to be an attempt to declare a trust of land but your marks will be increased if you discuss whether this is a declaration of trust anyway. Isabel has not actually used the word 'trust' here, so you can make use of your knowledge of certainty of intention to create a trust (see Chapter 3).

Assuming that it is a declaration of trust, then does it comply with the requirements of section 53(1)(b) LPA 1925? Clearly not, as it is not in writing or evidenced by writing. Therefore, the declaration is not void but cannot be enforced against Isabel's estate.

£20,000 in the bank account. The same points also apply here: is there an actual declaration of trust? If there is, then it is valid as section 53(1)(b) applies only to land.

Shares in the ABC Co.: Isabel is a beneficiary here and she is attempting to dispose of her equitable interest under the trust. Again, extra marks can be gained for spotting that, although she has not actually used the words 'dispose of my equitable interest', this is what she has actually done. Refer to section 53(1)(c) and note that it requires writing. This case is similar to *Grey* v *IRC* in that the beneficiary has directed the trustee to hold the property for another rather than make a direct disposition but, applying *Grey* v *IRC,* it is still caught by section 53(1)(c). Therefore, as she has not used writing, it is void and so Isabel's estate is still a beneficiary of the shares.

 Make your answer stand out

Show that you have:

- a thorough knowledge of the law which is clearly applied;
- paid close attention to the actual words of the relevant sections of the LPA;
- knowledge of the reasons why formalities are required – a mention of this would impress the examiner in an answer to a problem question.

READ TO IMPRESS

Battersby, G. (1979) Formalities for the disposition of equitable interests under trusts. 43 *Conv.* 17.

Garton, J. (2015) *Moffat's Trusts Law, Text and Materials,* 6th edn. Cambridge: Cambridge University Press.

Glister, J. (2014) Disclaimers and secret trusts. 1 *Conv.* 11.

Green, B. (1984) Grey, Oughtred and Vandervell – A contextual reappraisal. 47 *MLR* 385.

Liew, Y.K. (2012) *Rochefoucauld* v *Boustead,* in Mitchell, C. and Mitchell, P. (eds.) *Landmark Cases in Equity.* Oxford: Hart Publishing.

Milne, P. (1997) Oughtred revisited. 113 *LQR* 213.

Nolan, R. (1996) The triumph of technicality. 55 *CLJ* 436.

Swadling, W. (2009) The nature of the trust in *Rochefoucauld* v *Boustead,* in Mitchell, C. (ed.) *Constructive and Resulting Trusts.* Oxford: Hart Publishing.

www.pearsoned.co.uk/lawexpress

 Go online to access more revision support including quizzes to test your knowledge, sample questions with answer guidelines, printable versions of the topic maps, and more!

Constitution

Revision checklist

Essential points you should know:

- [ ] The methods of constituting a trust
- [ ] The principle in *Re Rose* and its application in more recent cases
- [ ] The position of beneficiaries and trustees where the trust is incompletely constituted
- [ ] Indirect constitution, as in *Re Ralli*
- [ ] The three ways in which equity may assist a volunteer

■ Topic map

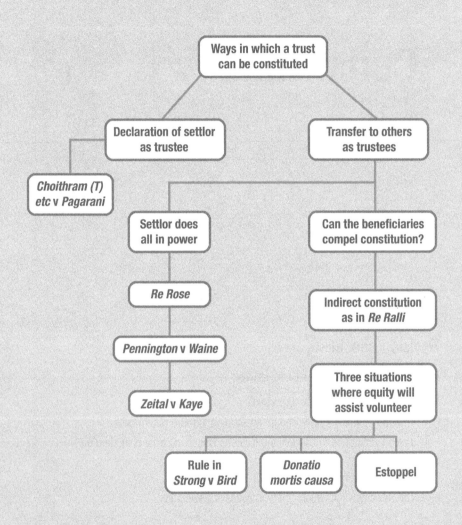

■ Introduction

Constitution of trusts is one of the major areas of equity and trusts and is likely to attract a question.

It can be a question on its own or, as the question can be combined with either or both certainties or formalities, you should always revise these areas carefully. There have been two cases, *Choithram (T) International SA* v *Pagarani* (2001) and *Pennington* v *Waine* (2002), which are likely to inspire questions. Note that *donatio mortis causa* may only be dealt with in outline in an equity course as it can appear in Succession.

ASSESSMENT ADVICE

Essay questions

A familiar essay question asks you to comment on the equitable maxim 'equity will not assist a volunteer' in the light of the law on constitution. Another could ask about the effect of *Pennington* v *Waine* (2002) on the requirements for constitution or deal with particular areas such as the three cases where equity may assist a volunteer.

Problem questions

Problem questions often involve a range of situations and ask you to decide whether the trust has been completely constituted in each. This is a good area for picking up marks as there will be a wide range of issues and you ought to be able to say something useful on at least some of them.

In many questions the person attempting the transfer (X) will have died and so the contest will be between the trustee/beneficiary, who will be claiming that the trust was properly constituted, and the person (Y) who was left the property under the will of X. Y will, of course, claim that as the trust was incompletely constituted, it still formed part of X's estate when he died and therefore passes to him. Do make a note of who Y is at the start of your answer and, as ever, always find a home for the property: do not leave it unallocated.

When answering a problem question, identify, in relation to each piece of property, what formalities were required to validly transfer it and whether they have been complied with. If not, then consider whether any of the exceptions outlined below apply.

■ Sample question

Could you answer this question? Below is a typical problem question that could arise on this topic. Guidelines on answering the question are included at the end of this chapter, while a sample essay question and guidance on tackling it can be found on the companion website.

PROBLEM QUESTION

Joshua suffered a haemorrhage and was rushed to hospital. His niece Belinda, his son Charles, his daughter Fiona and his friend Laura all visited him.

He said to Belinda: 'Here are the deeds to my house, The Laurels. As you know, I have always intended you to have it and now it is yours.'

He asked Charles to bring him the lease to his shop and wrote on it: 'I now declare that the benefit of this shop belongs to Charles absolutely.'

He told Fiona: 'You have been wonderful to me. You gave up your job to look after me and it was always understood between us that you would be rewarded. My seaside cottage is now yours.'

He said to Laura: 'I am not long for this world. Here is my post office savings book. This account is now yours. I have made out the necessary forms to put it into your name – here they are.'

That night Joshua died when the hospital was struck by lightning. His will appointed Fiona as his executrix.

Can you advise Belinda, Charles, Fiona and Laura as to any claims they might have to Joshua's property? Would it make any difference to your answer if Joshua had died six months later when playing tennis from an undetected heart condition?

■ Ways in which a trust can be constituted

📖 REVISION NOTE

Before looking at constitution, note the distinction between constitution and formalities, which was dealt with in Chapter 4. Questions may deal with both of these.

Look at these situations:

Example 5.1

Situation one	Situation two
Fred transfers £1,000 into a trust account in the name of his two trustees (Tim and Ted) to be held on the terms of a trust which he has declared for his two children, Mark and Charlotte.	Fred promises Tim and Ted that he will transfer £1,000 into the trust account for Mark and Charlotte but fails to do so.

The difference is obvious: in 'Situation one' Fred has transferred the money into the names of his trustees and so it is no longer Fred's money; in 'Situation two' Fred has promised to do so but no transfer has taken place.

In 'Situation one' there is a **constitution of trust**, but in 'Situation two' there is not.

KEY DEFINITION: Constitution of a trust

A trust is *constituted* when the legal title to the trust property is vested in the trustee(s).

A trust is *unconstituted* when the legal title to the trust property is not vested in the trustee(s).

✎ EXAM TIP

Always begin your answer to a problem question on constitution by identifying whether constitution has taken place. It almost certainly will not have done so, and you will then be able to continue by deciding whether there is any way in which the trust can be constituted.

Consider 'Situation two'. The trust has not been constituted, so what, if anything, can Mark and Charlotte do?

Your starting point must be the maxim that 'equity will not assist a **volunteer**' (e.g. see Lord Eldon in *Ellison* v *Ellison* (1802)).

KEY DEFINITION: Volunteer

A person who has not provided any consideration for a promise.

(Note that in equity the term 'consideration' is wider than in the common law of contract.)

Are Mark and Charlotte volunteers? Yes, as there is no evidence of their having provided consideration for Fred's promise to transfer £1,000 to Tim and Tom for their benefit.

The point that equity will not assist volunteers is not the end of the matter but is a good and clear way to start.

◼ Methods of constituting a trust

The authority for the two methods shown in Figure 5.1 is in the judgment of Turner LJ in *Milroy* v *Lord* (1862).

We will deal with 'Method one' now and concentrate on 'Method two' later.

Figure 5.1

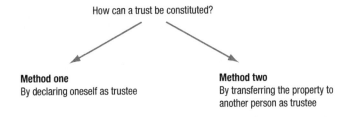

How can a trust be constituted?

Method one
By declaring oneself as trustee

Method two
By transferring the property to another person as trustee

Method one: declaration of settlor as trustee

Example 5.2

Jason has £1,000 in a bank account and says to his son, Christopher: 'I am now the trustee of this money for you.'

The effect is that a trust has been set up with Jason as trustee and Christopher as beneficiary (see Figure 5.2).

Figure 5.2

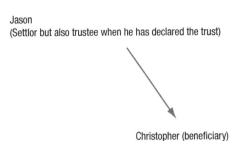

Jason
(Settlor but also trustee when he has declared the trust)

Christopher (beneficiary)

However, exam questions do not make the scenario as simple as this.

There have been a number of cases on this point and you should note the following carefully:

- *Jones* v *Lock* (1865)
- *Richards* v *Delbridge* (1874)
- *Paul* v *Constance* (1977).

In all of these cases the issue was whether words used by the settlor were enough to make him a trustee.

> 📖 **REVISION NOTE**
>
> Go back to Chapter 3 and revise the intention to create a trust.

An important case is as follows.

> **KEY CASE**
>
> *Choithram (T) International SA* v *Pagarani* [2001] 2 All ER 492 (PC)
>
> *Concerning: declaration of self as trustee*
>
> **Facts**
>
> X executed a trust deed which set up a charitable foundation and then said: 'I now give all my wealth to the foundation' (or words to this effect).
>
> **Legal principle**
>
> This was sufficient to constitute the trust as X was one of the trustees of the foundation and it did not matter that the property had not been vested in the other trustees. In addition, although the words used looked like an outright gift, they must have meant that X was constituting a trust.

 Make your answer stand out

This decision was controversial. Has it relaxed the law on constitution too much? Read Hopkins (2001) on this issue and note the remark of Lord Browne-Wilkinson in the above case: 'Although equity will not aid a volunteer, it will not strive officiously to defeat a gift.' What do you think he meant?

Method two: transfer to others as trustees

Figure 5.3

Example 5.3

See Example 5.2. Suppose that Jason had declared himself a trustee, not of £1,000 in his bank account but of his house.

This is 'Method one', and as this is freehold land one formality would be needed:

1. The actual declaration of trust would need to be in writing (s. 53(1)(b), LPA 1925 and see Chapter 4).

Suppose that 'Method two' was used and the scenario was as follows.

Example 5.4

Jason intends to transfer his house to Edith to hold on trust for Christopher.

We would now need two formalities:

1. as above, section 53(1)(b), LPA, must be complied with;
2. section 52(1), LPA, which requires transfers of freehold land to be by deed.

Settlor does all in his power to constitute the trust (i.e. to transfer the property to the trustees)

This can be another way to constitute a trust even though the requirements of *Milroy* v *Lord* are not satisfied.

Example 5.5

Anne is the owner of 5,000 shares in Midland Optical Illusion Co. Ltd, a private company. She wishes to transfer them to her daughter, Susan. However, a private company can refuse to register a transfer.

KEY CASE

Re Rose [1952] Ch 499 (HC)

Concerning: what is needed for the settlor to do all in his power to make the transfer?

Facts

The settlor executed a deed transferring shares in a private company to trustees.

Legal principle

It was enough if the settlor had done everything in his power to make the transfer binding, and this was when the deed was executed. Although directors of a private company have a discretion to refuse to register a transfer, at the moment when the deed was executed the settlor had done all in his power to make the transaction binding on him.

This was applied in *Mascall* v *Mascall* (1985) to a transfer of registered land: here it is the Land Registry that completes the transfer.

KEY CASE

Pennington v *Waine* [2002] EWCA Civ 227 (CA)

Concerning: what is needed to make a transfer binding on a person when another person or body needs to complete the transfer?

Facts

A donor had executed a form transferring shares in a private company to her nephew but had not delivered it to him; instead it had gone to the auditor of the company. The gift was completed, as it was not necessary for the form to be delivered to the nephew.

Legal principle

A gift can be deemed to be complete if it would have been unconscionable for the donor to change her mind at this point (Arden LJ).

 Make your answer stand out

This case, like *Choithram* (above), is seen as a controversial relaxation of the rules on constitution as the donor did not do all in her power to complete the transfer. Read more on it: see Garton (2003).

KEY CASE

Zeital v *Kaye* [2010] EWCA Civ 159

Concerning: application of the rule in Re Rose *where the transferor held only a beneficial interest*

Facts

Agents held shares in a company on trust for R. R gave S the transfer form relating to a share without adding her name as transferee.

Legal principle

R only held an equitable interest in the shares and so his actions could only transfer the equitable interest. He needed to declare himself a trustee of this interest for S or make a written assignment of his equitable interest to S in accordance with section 53(1)(c) of the Law of Property Act 1925. As he had done neither of these things, there was no transfer from R to S.

 Make your answer stand out

Refer to another recent case on this area, *Curtis* v *Pulbrook* [2011] EWHC 167, and to an article that discusses *Zeital* v *Kaye*: Griffiths (2010).

REVISION NOTE

Go to Chapter 4 and revise your knowledge of section 53(1)(c) LPA 1925.

Other formal requirements for transfer of property

Other property requires other formalities to transfer it: equitable interests need writing (s. 53(1)(c), LPA 1925; see Chapter 4); chattels need a deed of gift or the intention to give them or parting with possession; and shares need the appropriate transfer form and registration of the transferee as owner.

Can the beneficiaries compel constitution?

Equity will not assist a volunteer. A volunteer is a person who has not provided consideration. So, if the beneficiaries have not provided consideration, then equity will not assist them unless the situation is within the three exceptional situations dealt with below. It then becomes crucial to know what is meant by 'consideration'.

Consideration in equity has a wider meaning than at common law because equity also includes **marriage consideration**.

In equity this includes the husband and wife and the issue of the marriage.

Marriage consideration will appear when a settlement is made either before or after marriage and (this is the crucial point) in consideration of marriage, under which the settlor promises to settle property on his or her (future) husband or wife. If so, they can enforce the promise if it is not carried out and so can their issue (see *Pullan* v *Koe* (1913)). Does it now include a civil partnership?

Suppose that the beneficiaries have not given consideration but they are parties to a deed of covenant under which there is a promise to constitute a trust by settling property on them.

Note that:

- equity recognises marriage consideration; common law does not;
- common law recognises promises made in a deed (*Cannon* v *Hartley* (1949)); equity does not;
- common law remedy is damages; equitable remedy will probably be specific performance.

In addition, the Contracts (Rights of Third Parties) Act 1999 may change the answer.

Take some examples and see how these principles apply to them. Note that here we are considering only whether the beneficiary is able to enforce the promise. We will consider the position of the trustee later.

Let us assume that the Contracts (Rights of Third Parties) Act 1999 does not apply.

Example 5.6

John promises his fiancée, Miranda, that, in contemplation of his marriage to her, he will transfer £10,000 to Robert to hold on trust for her. He fails to do so.

Can Miranda enforce this promise?	Yes
In equity or common law?	Equity – marriage consideration

Therefore, equitable remedies apply, e.g. specific performance (SP).

Example 5.7

John promises Miranda, his girlfriend, that he will transfer £10,000 to Robert on trust for her but fails to do so.

Can Miranda enforce this promise?	No

Miranda is a volunteer – unlike in Example 5.6, there is no evidence of marriage consideration.

Example 5.8

John promises Miranda by a deed, to which John, Miranda and Robert are parties, that he will transfer £10,000 to Robert to hold on trust for her but fails to do so.

Can Miranda enforce the promise?	Not in equity

Equity does not enforce promises in a deed made without consideration – an example of the maxim that equity does not assist a volunteer, and Miranda has given no consideration.

However, common law will give a remedy for broken promises in a deed, so Miranda can claim damages.

KEY STATUTE

Contracts (Rights of Third Parties) Act 1999, section 1

Section 1 enables a person who is not a party to a contract to take the benefit of a contractual term in two cases:

(1) If the contract expressly provides that he or she may do so.
(2) If a term of the contract purports to confer a benefit – unless on a proper construction of the term it appears that it was not intended to be enforceable by the third party.

How could this affect the above situations?

- It applies only to contracts made on or after 11 May 2000.
- It will allow an action by a beneficiary where the contract or deed (the Act includes deeds – section 7(3)) between the settlor and the trustee expressly conferred a benefit on the beneficiary.

This means that, provided there was a contract and not just a promise, a beneficiary may be able to enforce the obligation to constitute a trust in his or her favour. So, the answer to Example 5.7 may be different, and in Example 5.8 the volunteer might be able to sue under this Act as well as at common law, although there is doubt as to whether specific performance can be obtained under the Act.

▉ Trustee's position where trust is incompletely constituted

What of Robert, the trustee in the above examples? Assuming that Miranda is unable to take action herself, can he do so on her behalf? The answer is probably no, although the cases do not give a definite answer: see, for example, *Re Pryce* (1917); *Re Kay* (1939); *Re Cook's Settlement Trusts* (1965).

▉ Indirect constitution of a trust

KEY CASE

Re Ralli's Will Trust [1964] Ch 288 (HC)

Concerning: indirect constitution of a trust

Facts

(Simplified) The trustee was also the executor under the will of the settlor/testator and the trust was held to be constituted.

Legal principle

A trust can be constituted if the trust property reaches the intended trustee in an indirect way (i.e. as in the above case, where the trustee was also the executor) and one which was not intended by the settlor.

✎ EXAM TIP

If the scenario has the same person as both the trustee under an unconstituted trust and as the executor under the settlor's will, then look carefully to see whether *Re Ralli* applies. This makes it easy to spot in an exam.

Three ways in which equity may assist a volunteer

> 📎 **EXAM TIP**
>
> These are exceptions to the principle that 'equity will not assist a volunteer'. Note that they deal with gifts, but they can also be relevant to attempts to constitute a trust.

1 Rule in *Strong* v *Bird*

> **KEY CASE**
>
> ***Strong* v *Bird* (1874) LR 18 Eq 315 (CA)**
>
> *Concerning: perfecting an incomplete gift (i.e. one that has been promised but not made)*
>
> **Facts**
> X had borrowed £1,100 from his stepmother but did not repay £900 of it. Her will appointed him as her executor.
>
> **Legal principle**
> Where there is an intention to make an immediate gift, or to release a debt, and that intention continues until the death of the donor, then the appointment of the donee as executor perfects the gift/releases the debt. Therefore, the debt of £900 owed by X to his stepmother was released.

> **Example 5.9**
>
> Pam promises Teresa that she will give Teresa her car. Pam then appoints Teresa as her executor. On Pam's death Teresa can claim the car.

Suppose that before her death Pam had told her daughter, Sophie, that she could borrow the car. Here the rule in *Strong* v *Bird* would not apply as there needs to be a continuing intention to make an immediate gift (*Re Gonin* (1979)) and clearly this cannot now be the case.

Does this rule also apply to **administrators** appointed under intestacy? See *Re Gonin* (1979) – a very useful case for exams.

2 *Donatio mortis causa* (DMC)

This exception applies where a gift is made:

- in contemplation of death. In *King* v *Dubrey* (2016) it was held that this requirement is not satisfied where an elderly donor is simply approaching the end of his or her natural life and that *Vallee* v *Birchwood* (2013), which had decided that this was sufficient, was wrong. See Cumber (2016).

■ where the subject matter of the gift, or the means of control of it, or some essential indication of title, was delivered to the donee;

■ where there was an intention to make the gift conditional on death.

Thus a DMC is in one way a legacy, to comply with the first two requirements but is also a lifetime gift, to comply with the third requirement.

A significant case is:

KEY CASE

Sen v *Hedley* [1991] Ch 425 (CA)

Concerning: can land be the subject of a DMC

Facts

The deceased was terminally ill and said to the claimant (a very close friend for many years): 'The house is yours, Margaret. You have the keys. They are in your bag. The deeds are in a steel box.'

Legal principle

There can be a valid DMC of land and there was a valid DMC here as all the requirements were satisfied.

Note that in *Koh Cheong Heng* v *Ho Yee Fong* (2011) the Singapore High Court held that, where title to land is registered, a DMC is also possible, but is not clear what could be handed over to represent delivery of the subject matter of the gift.

📖 REVISION NOTE

The effect of a DMC is that, pending the death of the donor, the property is held on a constructive trust for the donee (see *Sen* v *Hedley*). Check Chapter 8 and make sure that you are clear about the meaning of a constructive trust.

 Make your answer stand out

Research the Inheritance (Provision for Families and Dependants) Act 1975 and ask if a possible claim here would make reliance on a DMC unnecessary. This kind of thinking really boosts your marks!

3 Estoppel

Estoppel is a principle that appears in land law too, but it may arise here in the context of incomplete gifts, e.g. where a promise to put land in another's name is not put in the required formality – see *Dillwyn* v *Llewellyn* (1862). In this context it will be a case of proprietary *estoppel*. Estoppel is considered in more detail in Chapter 8. Note that in *King* v *Dubrey* there could not be an estoppel claim on the facts as there was no detrimental reliance; but still look at this issue even if the question appears to be on a DMC.

■ Putting it all together

Answer guidelines

See the problem question at the start of the chapter.

Approaching the question

Valid transfers by John? Check formalities. If not, DMC? Note that John died from a different reason than he thought he would. Estoppel? Note Fiona is executor.

Important points to include

- Belinda: no valid transfer. Here land involved and LPA 1925, section 52(1) must be complied with – deed required and no deed. Could be a DMC – note *Sen* v *Hedley* can have a DMC of land, but it appears to be an outright gift and not one conditional on death. Therefore, it fails, and the property remains in Joshua's estate. Title to the land appears to be unregistered. If it was registered how could there be a DMC: what is there to hand over?

- Charles: is this a declaration that Joshua now holds on trust for Charles? Older cases may be against this (e.g. see *Richards* v *Delbridge*), but note the more relaxed view taken in *Choithram*. If it is not a valid declaration of trust, then the property forms part of Joshua's estate.

- Fiona: possibility of a DMC but there is no delivery of any indication of title. Could be proprietary estoppel: set out the requirements for a valid estoppel but do not come to a definite conclusion – not enough evidence to decide.

- Laura: could be a DMC but again it looks like an outright gift. Apply *Pennington* v *Waine* and *Re Rose* and see whether it could be valid on the principle that Joshua has done all that he can to transfer title to the property.

- If Fiona is appointed executrix, then the gift to her is perfected – *Strong* v *Bird*.
- If Joshua died six months later when playing tennis, then he must have recovered from his original illness and so, if there were any valid DMCs, they would have been revoked.

 Make your answer stand out

This answer used the cases of *Choithram* and *Pennington,* but you will gain extra marks if you can show how the approach in earlier cases differed. In addition, the judges in the Court of Appeal in *Pennington* gave different reasons for their decisions; look at these and discuss them. You could also ask whether the recent case of *Zeital* v *Kaye* is evidence of a return to a stricter approach.

Finally, when discussing the DMC issue, you could refer to recent cases in this area (see above) and ask if this is evidence of a new approach.

READ TO IMPRESS

Cumber, H. (2016) Donationes mortis causa; a doctrine on its deathbed? 1 *Conv.* 56

Gardner, S. (2006) The remedial discretion in proprietary estoppel – again. 122 *LQR* 492.

Garton, J. (2003) The role of the trust mechanism in the rule in *Re Rose*. 87 *Conv.* 364.

Griffiths, G. (2010) Doing everything necessary – a recent manifestation of an ongoing issue. 4 *Conv.* 321.

Halliwell, M. (2003) Perfecting imperfect gifts and trusts: have we reached the end of the Chancellor's foot? 87 *Conv.* 192.

Hopkins, J. (2001) Constitution of trusts – a novel point. 60 *CLJ* 483.

www.pearsoned.co.uk/lawexpress

 Go online to access more revision support including quizzes to test your knowledge, sample questions with answer guidelines, printable versions of the topic maps, and more!

Secret and half-secret trusts

6

■ Topic map

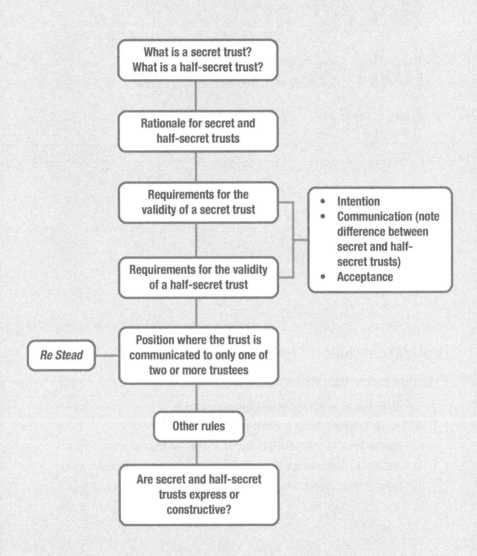

What is a secret trust?
What is a half-secret trust?

Rationale for secret and
half-secret trusts

Requirements for the
validity of a secret trust

- Intention
- Communication (note
  difference between
  secret and half-
  secret trusts)
- Acceptance

Requirements for the validity
of a half-secret trust

Re Stead

Position where the trust is
communicated to only one of
two or more trustees

Other rules

Are secret and half-secret
trusts express or
constructive?

A printable version of this topic map is available from www.pearsoned.co.uk/lawexpress

▇ Introduction

There is often a problem question on these trusts.

In addition, this topic is an excellent illustration of a familiar maxim of equity: *equity will not allow a statute to be used as an engine of fraud* and so it is useful for essay questions.

Secret trusts form one of the four interlocking topics in trusts law and you should be prepared for a question that involves one or more of these topics. This is a reminder of what they are:

- Three certainties
- Formalities
- Secret trusts
- Constitution.

A question on secret trusts will not be likely to involve constitution but it could certainly involve the others. If so, secret trusts will be the main issue, but you will also be expected to deal with the others.

ASSESSMENT ADVICE

Essay questions

An essay question on secret and half-secret trusts could involve either:

1. a question on the theoretical basis of these trusts; or
2. a question based on one of the maxims: equity will not allow a statute to be used as an engine of fraud (the statute here is the Wills Act 1837) or equity looks to the intent rather than the form, i.e. equity looks at the intention to create a trust rather than whether the formalities have been complied with (here, those in the Wills Act 1837).

The moral is to think clearly about just why these trusts should be enforced and be able to weigh up the opposing arguments.

In an essay question you should also mention the research by Meager, R. (2003) showing that secret trusts are important in practice.

Problem questions

Problems will require you to say whether the trust is valid and so you must be able to apply the tests for the validity of a secret and half-secret trust. Almost certainly the problem will involve one or both of the decisions in *Re Keen* (1937) and *Re Stead* (1900). If you decide that the trust is valid, there will be subsidiary points to watch for: for example, did trustees/beneficiaries witness the will? Is it a trust of land? You will also need to bear in mind the requirements of certainty, as explained above.

■ Sample question

Can you answer this question? Below is a typical problem question that could arise on this topic. Guidelines on answering the question are included at the end of the chapter while a sample essay question and guidance on tackling it can be found on the companion website.

PROBLEM QUESTION

Jennifer is aged 87 and had been told by her doctor that she may not have long to live. She has substantial savings, together with her house, The Laurels, which she does not wish to leave to any of her family, whom she dislikes, and so she explains the problem to her friends Mabel and Fanny. She tells them both that she intends to make them beneficiaries under her will but that she will let them know what to do with their bequests later. They are both puzzled but agree to help if they can. Jennifer telephones Mabel later that day and they have a long conversation.

Jennifer executes her will on 1 February, three days after she had spoken to Mabel and Fanny. In it, she leaves £50,000 and The Laurels to Mabel to be used for 'the purposes which we have discussed' and £100,000 to Fanny. Mabel and Fanny were witnesses to the will. The local hospital is named as the residuary beneficiary.

Later that day, Jennifer gave Mabel an envelope on which were written the words: 'This contains important instructions. Open immediately on my death but not before.'

On 3 February Jennifer wrote to Fanny and told her that, of the £100,000, £90,000 should be held on trust for all the employees and their relatives of Barset College to be distributed among them at Fanny's discretion. The other £10,000 is a gift to Fanny in memory of the good times that she and Jennifer shared together. Fanny received this letter on 4 February.

Jennifer died on 5 February. Mabel finds that The Laurels is to be held on trust for Alf, Jennifer's son, and the £50,000 is to be held on trust for Jack, an old friend of Jennifer. However, Jack predeceased Jennifer.

Advise Mabel and Fanny on whether the trusts are valid and, if not, for whose benefit the property should be held.

■ The distinction between secret and half-secret trusts

Example 6.1	**Example 6.2**
John wishes to leave £10,000 to his girlfriend Fifi but does not want his wife to know of this, as she is unaware of his relationship with Fifi. Accordingly, he decides to leave the property to someone who will hold it on trust to carry out his wishes.	Susan wishes to make a will as she is going into hospital for a major operation, but she cannot decide who to leave her property to.
John's will reads: 'I leave £10,000 to Steve.'	Susan's will reads: 'I leave all my property to Deborah on the trusts which I have declared to her.'
This is a *secret trust* as the will does not disclose either the existence or the details of the trust. Ask the question: on reading the will, would anyone know that there was a trust? If not, the trust is secret.	This is a *half-secret trust,* as although the will discloses the existence of a trust, it does not disclose the details of it.

KEY DEFINITION: Secret trust

Where the will or other document does not disclose the existence of the trust.

KEY DEFINITION: Half-secret trust

Where the will or other document discloses the existence of the trust but not the details.

✎ EXAM TIP

If you are faced with a problem question on secret trusts in the exam, first look at the words of the will, as these will tell you whether the trust is secret or half-secret. The rules for each are different in some respects and so it is vital to be clear at the outset which category the trust falls into. Note *Re Freud* (2014) which considered the distinction between secret and half-secret trusts.

> **✎ EXAM TIP**
>
> The words used by the settlor should be looked at carefully to see that certainty of intention to create a trust is disclosed (e.g. in the will). If it is, then the trust will be half-secret.
>
> If you are in doubt whether the words disclose a secret or a half-secret trust, you should answer for both, although it may be that the court would decide that there was enough evidence of an obligation for there to be a half-secret trust. In *Blackwell* v *Blackwell* (1929) the will used the word 'purposes' and this was enough for a half-secret trust.

■ Rationale for secret and half-secret trusts

The fraud rationale

This is that secret trusts must be enforced by equity to prevent fraud.

> **Make your answer stand out**
>
> Look at the judgment of Lord Westbury in *McCormick* v *Grogan* (1869) for a clear statement of the fraud rationale.

> **✎ EXAM TIP**
>
> Secret trusts are excellent examples of the maxim 'equity will not allow a statute to be used as an engine of fraud' and an essay question may ask you to discuss this maxim. Make a list of examples of this maxim, and others you encounter, to be cited in answers. See Chapters 4 and 8 for further examples.

The intention rationale

This is that equity enforces half-secret trusts to give effect to the intentions of the settlor.

> **Make your answer stand out**
>
> See the judgment of Lord Buckmaster in *Blackwell* v *Blackwell* (1929) for a clear statement of the intention rationale.

Secret trusts normally arise in the context of gifts by will, and these form the main part of this chapter. They can also arise when an *inter vivos* gift is made. An exam question will almost certainly involve gifts by will but an answer to an essay question will be improved by a discussion of secret trusts arising *inter vivos*. Could one also arise on an intestacy where the person entitled agrees to hold what they receive on a secret trust? See *Stickland* v *Aldridge* (1804).

■ Requirements for the validity of a secret trust

The requirements are as follows:

- the *intention* of the testator to create a trust (together with the trust property being certain and the objects of the trust satisfying the test for certainty of objects);
- *communication* of that intention to the intended trustees in the lifetime of the testator;
- *acceptance* of the trust by the intended trustees either expressly or by acquiescence.

See *Ottaway* v *Norman* (1972) where these were clearly stated.

Intention, subject matter and objects

We saw above that certainty of intention is relevant in deciding whether the trust was secret or half-secret. In addition, all the three certainties must be present for both secret and half-secret trusts.

Suppose that Susan's will said: 'I leave all my property to Deborah for the purposes which I have indicated to her.' This may look like a half-secret trust at first sight but the words 'purposes which I have indicated to her' do not clearly disclose the existence of a trust. Your knowledge of the rules on certainty of intention will be needed here.

Look at the words used in *Gold* v *Hill* (1998) where there was sufficient intention.

Communication

Always check that you have found a home for the property. If there is no valid trust, decide where it will go. Where the secret trust was not communicated, it will then be a gift to the intended trustee (donee).

KEY CASE

Wallgrave v *Tebbs* (1855) 2 K & J 313 (HC)

Concerning: communication of secret trusts

Facts

The facts of this case do not aid an understanding of the legal principle.

Legal principle

In cases of secret trusts the trust must be communicated during the lifetime of the testator; so here the intended trustee took the property absolutely, as there was no trust.

Communication will be valid where the testator delivers a sealed envelope to the intended trustee with the direction: 'Not to be opened until after my death' (*Re Keen* (1937)). However, the intended trustee must know that the envelope contains details of the trust and it must be handed to her during the lifetime of the testator.

A halfway situation

The testator tells the intended trustee that she is to hold the property on trust but does not communicate the details of the trust. Here the intended trustee cannot take the property beneficially as she knows that she is a trustee; she therefore holds it on a resulting trust for the testator's estate (*Re Boyes* (1884)).

Acceptance

The intended trustee must accept the trust either expressly or by acquiescence, and so silence will be enough for acceptance – contrast the position in contract. In *Moss* v *Cooper* (1861) Wood VC referred to 'acquiescence either by words of consent or silence'.

■ Requirements for the validity of a half-secret trust

✎ EXAM TIP

The only difference between the requirements for the validity of a half-secret trust and a secret trust is the rules on communication. Thus, you already know two of the three requirements.

In the case of half-secret trusts, intention to create a trust will appear in the will itself.

✎ EXAM TIP

An exam question may not clearly indicate whether the trust is secret or half-secret. In the exam question the words were 'for the purposes which we have discussed'. The word 'trust' was not mentioned but the word 'purposes' probably indicates a trust, or it may not. You will thus gain extra marks by answering on the basis that it is half-secret (which it probably is) and then secret (which it might just be).

Communication in half-secret trusts

This is a favourite area for exam questions because the law is uncertain. There are two possible rules:

■ Rule one (which is probably the law): *Re Keen* (1937): communication must be before the date of the execution of the will (*Re Keen* (1937)). This was confirmed in *Re Freud* (2014).

If this is the rule, then the difference between the two types of trust can be seen in Figure 6.1.

Figure 6.1

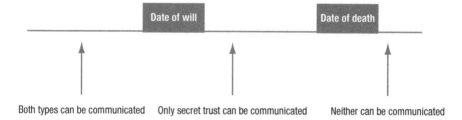

Both types can be communicated   Only secret trust can be communicated   Neither can be communicated

■ Rule two: if the will states a time of communication, then the trust must be communicated at that time. This rule also arises from *Re Keen* and the fact that there are two rules arises from the judgment of Lord Wright in *Re Keen*.

KEY CASE

Re Keen [1937] Ch 236 (CA)

Concerning: communication of a half-secret trust

Facts

The testator left £10,000 to trustees to hold on trust and to be disposed of by them among such persons, etc., as may 'be notified by me to them during my lifetime'.   ▶

Legal principle

- The words 'to be notified by me' indicated an intention to make future communications and this was invalid as communication must be before the will.

- The actual communication was before the will and this conflicted with the words to 'be notified'.

A final point: Where a codicil is later added to a will, this 'republishes the will' so that the date of the will is now the date of the codicil. This can affect the rules on communication.

Example 6.1

Date of will: 1 January

Date of communication: 1 February

Communication is too late if 'Rule one' is applied.

Date of codicil: 1 March

Therefore:

Date of will is now: 1 March

Communication is valid

Where the half-secret trust is not validly communicated, the property is held on a resulting trust for the residuary beneficiaries (e.g. the hospital in the exam question).

■ Position where the trust is communicated to only one of two or more trustees

KEY CASE

Re Stead [1900] 1 Ch 237 (HC)

Concerning: communication of a secret trust to some but not all intended trustees

Facts

The facts of this case do not aid an understanding of the legal principle.

Legal principle

- Where communication is to one of two joint tenants and this takes place *before* the will, then both joint tenants are bound.

- Where communication is to one of two joint tenants *after* the will, then only the one to whom the trust is communicated is bound.
- Where communication is to one of two tenants in common, then only the one to whom the trust is communicated is bound.

Example 6.2

Jason leaves £10,000 to Mark and Anthony. Before Jason executed the will he told Mark, but not Anthony, that he wanted the £10,000 to be held for the benefit of his daughter, Mary.

Mark and Anthony are joint tenants, as there are no words of severance, and so they are both bound. If the gift had been to Mark and Anthony in equal shares, they would then have been tenants in common and only Mark would have been bound. He would hold £5,000 on trust for Mary and Anthony would take the other £5,000 beneficially.

✎ EXAM TIP

It is unlikely that the distinction between tenants in common and joint tenants will involve your learning fine points of distinction between them. Look for words of severance: if they are there, the gift is to tenants in common; if they are not there, the gift is to joint tenants.

✓ Make your answer stand out

Refer to the criticism of this rule by Perrins (1972).

✎ EXAM TIP

For extra marks learn why this rule is felt to be unsatisfactory and what might replace it.

■ Other rules

These are as follows:

 Where there is an addition to the trust this must be communicated, e.g. if an additional sum is to be held on trust (*Re Cooper (Colin)* (1939)).

- Where a beneficiary under a secret trust witnesses the will, this does not affect the gift as the trust is outside (*dehors*) the will (*Re Young* (1951)).
- Where a person is named as trustee in a half-secret trust, and also witnesses it, this will not affect the trust as he or she is not named as a beneficiary but a trustee.
- Where a person is a trustee under a secret trust and witnesses the will, then that person cannot take the property as he or she appears in the will to be a beneficiary.
- Where a person attempts to disclaim the legacy that he agreed to hold on a secret trust it may be that the secret trust fails because legal title never vests in the secret trustee. However, it may be that the disclaimer should not be allowed as the secret trustee is under an obligation to accept the legacy. The point is undecided but see Glister (2014).
- Where a beneficiary under a secret or half-secret trust dies before the testator, the gift does not lapse but passes to the beneficiary's estate (*Re Gardner* (1920)). Had the gift been in a will, then in most cases the gift would have lapsed.
- There is doubt as to whether a person can bring evidence to show that he or she was intended to benefit under a secret or half-secret trust. In *Re Rees* (1950) it was held that this was not possible, but in *Re Tyler's Fund Trusts* (1967) it was suggested that such evidence is admissible.
- In *Re Freud* (2014) the will contained a bequest to the testator's solicitor and it was recognised that 'one reasonable explanation for a clause which confers a beneficial gift on a solicitor is that the testator intended to impose a fully secret trust'.
- The death of the secret trustee before the death of the testator causes the trust to fail as the gift to the trustee lapses. But if the trust is half-secret, then the trust can be valid as the will itself indicates a trust.

 Make your answer stand out

Read Evans (2014) who considers the rule that a solicitor who prepared a will must give evidence about its contents. If the will contained a half-secret trust it would then no longer be half secret.

! Don't be tempted to . . .

Be sure to mention that the decision in *Re Gardner* is often felt to be wrong as, at the date of the beneficiary's death, the trust was not constituted. This can happen only on the beneficiary's death.

■ Are secret and half-secret trusts express or constructive?

This point is important if the trust concerns land, as in the sample question. The rule is probably that a secret trust is 'constructive' as it is imposed to prevent fraud. A half-secret trust is probably 'express' as it is declared on the will.

This means that secret trusts of land need not be in writing, as writing is not necessary in constructive trusts of land (s. 53(2), LPA 1925); but half-secret trusts as express trusts are governed by section 53(1)(b), LPA 1925, which requires trusts of land other than resulting and constructive trusts to be evidenced by writing.

> 📖 **REVISION NOTE**
>
> Go back to Chapter 4 and check that you are clear on the formalities rules.

■ Putting it all together

Answer guidelines

See the problem question at the start of the chapter.

Approaching the question

Problem questions in this area usually contain a number of different issues, giving plenty of opportunity to gain a really good mark. However, it is essential to have a very clear and logical structure to your answer, otherwise you could get your points in the wrong order with disastrous effects on your marks. Make a plan of your answer and stick to it.

Important points to include

Trust to Mabel

Take the words 'for the purposes of'. Do they indicate a trust or not? An average answer will say that they do, which is probably the case, and this will mean that:

■ there is definitely intention to create a trust;
■ this is definitely a half-secret trust. ▶

An excellent answer will explain that the words 'on trust' are not used and so there is the possibility that:

- there is no intention, unless the conversation in the opening paragraph indicates sufficient intention;
- even if there is intention, which is probably the case, the trust may be secret.

If there is some doubt, then proceed for both types:

- On the basis that the trust is half-secret, there is intention, as indicated in the will, but communication is doubtful. The will states that the gift to Mabel is to be 'used for the purposes which we have discussed', which indicates a past communication. In fact, communication to Mabel is by an envelope which is not to be opened until Jennifer's death and the envelope is given to Mabel on the same day that the will is executed, but later.
- Under 'Rule one' communication appears to be too late but, as we saw above, *Re Keen* also established that communication could be a sealed envelope not to be opened until the testator's death provided that the testator knows that the envelope contains the details of the trust. Here the words 'important instructions' could be taken as indicating that the envelope does contain details of a trust, but it is not definite. The fact that communication is later in the day can probably be overlooked, but the point is not decided.
- Under 'Rule two' communication is probably invalid as the will says 'the purposes which we have discussed', unless the initial discussion in the first paragraph can be taken as communication, which must be doubtful.
- There is probably valid communication on the basis of *Re Keen* but an excellent answer would also point out that if 'Rule two' applies, then communication is not valid as the time of communication conflicts with the will. However, there is also the long telephone conversation between Jennifer and Mabel. An excellent answer would point out that this may have contained communication.
- On the basis that the trust is secret, there is valid communication as the handing over of the envelope amounts to communication before the death of the testator.
- If there is no valid communication, then Mabel will take on a resulting trust for the estate (the residuary beneficiary – the hospital). If communication is valid, then on we go.
- Is there a valid acceptance? There is no express acceptance, but it can be implied (*Moss* v *Cooper* (1861)) and after the initial conversation the long telephone conversation might have contained an acceptance.
- The trust concerns land. If it is half-secret, then it is express, and under section 53(1)(b), LPA 1925 the trust of The Laurels must be in writing. The bare details are in the will, which is, of course, written and, if this is sufficient, then the requirements are

satisfied. An excellent answer would point out that a failure to comply with section 53(1)(b) renders the trust unenforceable but not void.

■ If the trust is valid, the death of Jack will not cause the trust to fail and the gift to him will go to his estate (*Re Gardner*). (A good answer would say that this case is considered doubtful.)

Trust to Fanny

This is secret and appears valid: communication is before Jennifer's death, intention appears from the will (use of word 'trust' and acceptance can be implied).

Two problems arise:

1. Does the gift to employees, etc. satisfy the test of certainty of objects (*McPhail* v *Doulton* (1971) – see Chapter 3)? If not, it is a resulting trust for the estate – in this case the hospital.

2. Can Fanny adduce evidence that she was intended to be a beneficiary? Consider *Re Rees* and *Re Tyler's Fund Trusts.*

 Make your answer stand out

Pay very close attention to the actual words used in the trust. See the discussion above on whether there is any possibility that the trust to Mabel could be a secret trust.

READ TO IMPRESS

Critchley, P. (1999) Instruments of fraud: testamentary dispositions and secret trusts. 115 *LQR* 631.

Evans, S. (2014) Should professionally drafted half-secret trusts be extinct after *Larke* v *Nugus*? 3 *Conv.* 229.

Glister, J. (2014) Disclaimers and secret trusts. 1 *Conv.* 11

Meager, R. (2003) Secret trusts: do they have a future? 67 *Conv.* 203.

Perrins, B. (1972) Can you keep half a secret? 88 *LQR* 225.

www.pearsoned.co.uk/lawexpress

 Go online to access more revision support including quizzes to test your knowledge, sample questions with answer guidelines, printable versions of the topic maps, and more

Resulting trusts

Revision checklist

Essential points you should know:

- [ ] The distinction between express trusts and resulting/constructive trusts
- [ ] The theories that explain the basis of resulting trusts
- [ ] When a resulting trust arises where property is put into the name of another, and why this is so
- [ ] When a presumption of advancement arises and the significance of this today
- [ ] When a resulting trust can arise where the beneficial interest is not disposed of
- [ ] The importance of the *Quistclose* case

■ Topic map

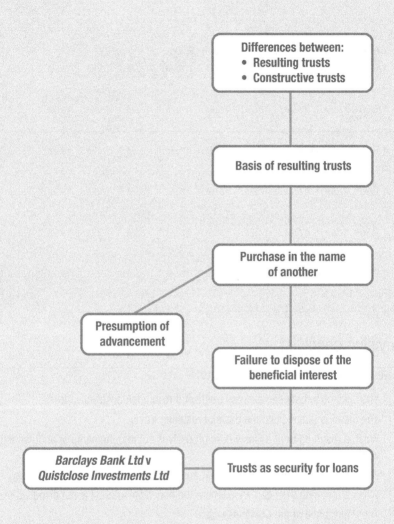

■ Introduction

This chapter and the next, on constructive trusts, should be considered together.

This is because:

■ there is a clear dividing line between express trusts, on the one hand, and resulting and constructive trusts on the other (see below). You may get a question on this point;

■ in some cases, and especially those involving trusts of the home, there can be uncertainty whether the trust should be classified as *resulting* or *constructive*. Trusts of the home are dealt with in Chapter 8.

ASSESSMENT ADVICE

Essay questions

This is a likely area for essays that could be on:

■ the basis of resulting trusts. This area is dealt with below and you should ensure that you understand the various theories, making sure that you can explain the basic idea behind them. You should then move on to relating the theories to the cases;

■ the basis of *Quistclose* trusts;

■ both resulting and constructive trusts, looking at their common features and how they differ.

Problem questions

A problem question could link with material on constructive trusts, an obvious area being trusts of the home, or deal with *Quistclose* trusts.

■ Sample question

Could you answer this question? Below is a typical essay question that could arise on this topic. Guidelines on answering the question are included at the end of the chapter, whilst a sample problem question and guidance on tackling it can be found on the companion website.

ESSAY QUESTION

'Resulting trusts are a rag-bag of different situations with no clear principle to explain them.'

Do you agree?

▮ Differences between express trusts and resulting and constructive trusts

The common feature of both resulting and constructive trusts is that, unlike express trusts, they are not created by the express agreement of the parties as evidenced in a trust deed, or some other writing, or – except in the case of trusts of land or an interest in land (s. 53(1)(b), LPA 1925) – orally. One possible exception is a secret trust (see Chapter 6) which is generally considered to be constructive but does arise from agreement.

> ### 📖 REVISION NOTE
>
> Go back to Chapter 6 and make sure that you are clear about what a secret trust is.

Garton (2015: 605–6) sets out these distinctions between express trusts on the one hand, and resulting and constructive (sometimes collectively called 'imputed') trusts on the other:

- ▮ *Functional.* Express trusts are often employed as a planning device; but imputed trusts are ways of resolving disputes over ownership or entitlement to property.
- ▮ *Formal.* Express trusts must comply with certain formalities such as section 53(1)(b), LPA 1925. Imputed trusts are not affected by these formalities (s. 53(2), LPA 1925).

We could also point to a substantive distinction. Express trusts arise because of some expression of intention by a property owner, but imputed trusts arise by operation of some legal rule. However, this particular distinction breaks down in cases of disputes over the family home, where intention plays a significant role.

> ### 📖 REVISION NOTE
>
> Go back to Chapter 4 and check that you know and understand what section 53(1)(b), section 53(1)(c) and section 53(2), LPA 1925 say.

The above points could form an excellent framework for an answer to an exam question that asks you to discuss the differences between express trusts on the one hand, and resulting and constructive trusts on the other.

■ Resulting trusts

Basis of resulting trusts

The idea behind **resulting trusts** is strange: a person (X) gives property to another (Y) and then Y ends up holding it on trust for X.

KEY DEFINITION: Resulting trust

The beneficial interest results to, or jumps back to, the settlor who created the trust. The basis of an action founded on a resulting trust is, therefore, that one is seeking to recover one's own property.

Theories to explain the basis of resulting trusts

1   Megarry J in *Re Vandervell's Trusts (No. 2)* (1974) – two types of resulting trust:

Automatic	Presumed
This has nothing to do with the intentions of the settlor (e.g. where no certainty of objects) – see Chapter 3.	Where property is transferred to another for no consideration (i.e. nothing given or promised in return) but no words of gift are used. Megarry J felt that these did arise from the presumed intention of the settlor. This chapter contains examples of these.

Chambers (1997: 47) points out, however, that *all* resulting trusts are concerned with the intentions of the settlor as one reason why they arise is that the settlor does not intend the property to go to the transferee as a gift but instead intends it to be held on trust. A more fundamental objection is pointed out by Swadling (2008): nothing is automatic in the law. The trust does not arise automatically but because the courts say that it does.

2   Lord Browne-Wilkinson in *Westdeutsche Landesbank Girozentrale* v *Islington LBC* (1996): resulting trusts arise from the common intention of the parties.

Example 7.1

Joan transfers £100 to Penny to hold on trust but fails to specify the trusts. The £100 is held on trust by Penny for Joan.

 Make your answer stand out

Swadling (2008) points out that intention arises in a negative sense only as the initial intention, in the above example, was for Penny to hold the £100 on trust; there is therefore only a presumed intention of a resulting trust as the first intention could not be carried out. In addition, can we just assume that this was the intention?

In *Re Vinogradoff* (1935) the testatrix had transferred an £800 War Loan which was in her own name into the joint names of herself and her four-year-old daughter. After the testatrix died, it was held that even though the daughter had not been appointed a trustee she still held it on a resulting trust for the testatrix's estate. The fundamental point is that the court did not say that it came to this decision because of the testatrix's intentions.

3 Chambers (1997): all resulting trusts should be considered as arising from the presumption of *the lack of any intention* by the transferor to pass any beneficial interest to the transferee when the transferee has not provided the entire consideration for the property. Thus, in the example above, the resulting trust operates because Joan did not intend to benefit Penny.

4 Swadling (2008): Chambers' view is wrong. Swadling's argument is that the word 'presumption' needs clarification. He argues that a true presumption arises where proof of one fact generates proof of another without the need for further evidence. In the case of resulting trusts, where the transferor puts property into the name of another, the evidence is that equity originally rested the presumption on evidence that the transferor declared a trust in his own favour. 'Automatic' resulting trusts, according to Swadling, seem to have no clear foundation. It is usually considered that, on any transfer, only *the legal* interest passes to the transferee. Where the resulting trust arises from that transfer, a new equitable interest arises which is held for the transferor (see Chambers (above)). Look at the *Quistclose* case (below) to test this idea.

 Don't be tempted to . . .

Don't forget to consider what happens to the beneficial interest.

■ Cases where a resulting trust can arise

Voluntary conveyances

The basic equitable rule is that where there is a voluntary conveyance of property (i.e. a gift) there is a presumption that the other person holds it on a resulting trust for the purchaser.

> ### Example 7.2
>
> X buys a house and puts it in Y's name. There is a presumption that Y holds it on trust for X. This can be rebutted by proof that a gift was intended (see *Dyer* v *Dyer* (1788)).

In *Hodgson* v *Marks* (1971) the owner transferred her house into the name of her lodger and it was held that there was a resulting trust in her favour.

Trusts of the home may come into this category. See Chapter 8 for the views of Lord Neuberger in *Stack* v *Dowden* (2007) and the decision in *Laskar* v *Laskar* (2008) on the applicability of resulting trusts to deciding the beneficial interests in the home.

Where there is a voluntary conveyance of land (i.e. the actual transfer is by gift) then section 60(3) of the LPA 1925 provides that a resulting trust for the grantor (i.e. the transferor) is not to be implied merely because the land is not expressed to be conveyed on trust for him. The effect of this has been debated, but in *Lohia* v *Lohia* (2001) the High Court held that in effect it means what it says: where land is conveyed as a gift then there is no presumption of a resulting trust.

KEY CASE

Prest v *Petrodel Resources Ltd* [2013] UKSC 34

Concerning: when a resulting trust arises on a voluntary transfer.

Facts

The case involved ancillary relief proceedings following divorce where the wife (W) alleged that her then husband (H) had a beneficial interest in eight homes. He had transferred the ownership of these to companies which he controlled in return for nominal sums. If W's claim succeeded, then H could be ordered to transfer the homes to her.

Legal principle

No explanation had been given for why the homes had been transferred to the companies with only nominal consideration and so the presumption that the companies held them on a resulting trust for H would apply and so W could claim them. See Hsiao (2017).

Presumption of advancement

In contrast to the example above – where there is a presumption of a resulting trust – here there is a presumption that the person making the transfer intends an outright gift (an advancement).

The situations where a presumption can arise were rather old-fashioned (e.g. they applied where a husband transfers property to his wife but not vice versa, and to advancements by a father (but not a mother) to his children). However, in *Pecore* v *Pecore* (2007) the Canadian Supreme Court held that they could also apply to an advancement by a mother. The cases also held that the presumption ceases when the child becomes an independent adult.

The presumption of advancement was abolished by section 199 of the Equality Act 2010, but this does not apply to things done before section 199 came into force. This means that the presumption will be relevant for some time as litigation can occur many years after a purchase (Glister, 2010). Note: At January 2018, section 199 was not yet in force.

Meanwhile, a clear statement of when presumptions of advancement can apply is in the judgment of Phillips MR in *Lavelle* v *Lavelle* (2004): 'Where there is no close relationship between A and B, there will be a presumption that A does not intend to part with the beneficial interest in the property and B will take the legal title under a resultant trust for A. Where, however, there is a close relationship between A and B, such as father and child, a presumption of advancement will apply. The implication will be that A intended to give the beneficial interest in the property to B and the transaction will take effect accordingly.'

An interesting area is where the presumption of a resulting trust appears to collide with the maxim that 'equity does not assist a person with unclean hands'.

KEY CASE

Tinsley v *Milligan* [1994] 1 AC 340 (HL)

Concerning: transfers of property for unlawful purposes

Facts

A house was bought with money provided by two women (X and Y) but was put into the name of X only so that Y could (fraudulently) claim housing benefit. Y claimed that the property was held for her on a resulting trust by virtue of her contributions.

Legal principle

The issue was the conduct that Y had to rely on to support her claim of a resulting trust. If it was her fraud, then she could not claim a resulting trust, in view of the principle stated above. However, here she only had to rely on her contributions to the purchase price, and so her claim succeeded as her fraud was, as a matter of evidence, irrelevant.

Make your answer stand out

This decision of the House of Lords has been strongly criticised. Look, for example, at Buckley (1994), but also note a contrary view expressed by Enonchong (1995). You should also look at the judgments of the Court of Appeal, which differed from those of the majority of the House of Lords: see *Tinsley* v *Milligan* [1992] Ch 310 CA. However, *Tinsley* has been applied in a case of common intention constructive trust (*O'Kelly* v *Davies* (2014).

 Make your answer stand out

Consultation Paper 154, published by the Law Commission in 1999 (*Illegal Transactions: The Effect of Illegality on Contracts and Trusts*), recommends that the courts should be given discretion in these cases, but also sets five criteria at paragraph 1.19. Look at these carefully.

Note also *Tinker* v *Tinker* (1970).

Failure to dispose of the beneficial interest

Example 7.3

Re Osoba (deceased) (1979): a trust was set up to maintain two women and to educate a third. After the death of the first two and the completion of the education of the third, the surplus went absolutely to the third. Yet in *Re Abbott* (1982) a fund to maintain two ladies which had a surplus went to the subscribers to it. Note also *Re Gillingham Bus Disaster Fund* (1959) in Chapter 9.

📖 **REVISION NOTE**

Look at Chapter 9 where this issue is considered in connection with failure of charitable trusts. Compare the rules when a charitable fund fails with those when a non-charitable fund fails.

Trusts as security for loans

KEY CASE

Barclays Bank Ltd v Quistclose Investments Ltd [1970] AC 567 (HL)

Concerning: when a loan can be held on a resulting trust for the lender

Facts

Quistclose lent money to a company (Rolls Razor) for the sole purpose of enabling it to pay dividends, and this money was held in a separate bank account. The company went into liquidation before the dividend was paid.

Legal principle

Where a loan is made for a specific purpose which fails, then a resulting trust may arise for the lender, in this case Quistclose. The effect is to give the lender priority over the borrower's creditors if, as here, the borrower goes into liquidation. Lord Wilberforce held that there were two trusts: a primary trust for the payment of identifiable beneficiaries followed by a secondary (resulting) trust in favour of the lender if the primary purpose fails.

KEY CASE

Re Farepak Food and Gifts Ltd (in administration) [2006] EWHC 3272 (Ch)

Concerning: possible application of the Quistclose principle

Facts

Under a Christmas hamper scheme operated by Farepak, customers placed orders for hampers with Farepak's agents who then passed them on to Farepak. Farepak decided to cease trading. Before it went into administration the directors attempted to 'ring fence' money that was received by Farepak so that it could be returned to customers. They did this by a declaration of trust; but did it actually create a trust?

Legal principle

The *Quistclose* principle could not apply because the money had been received by the Farepak agents (not Farepak) and, when it was received, there was no suggestion that it was to be kept separate from other money. Thus, there could be no *Quistclose* trust as there was, in effect, no trust property. There could only have been such a trust had the money from customers been kept in a separate fund so that it could not be touched until the customers had received their hampers.

The *Re Farepak* case is also relevant to express trusts (Chapter 3) and constructive trusts (Chapter 8). It could form an excellent illustration, in an essay question, of the modern application of the law of trusts.

Twinsectra v *Yardley* [2002] UKHL 12

Concerning: application of the Quistclose *principle*

Facts

T lent £1 million to Y for Y to buy property but Y spent nearly one-third of it on other purposes and T sued for its return. The money had actually been advanced to S, Y's solicitor, who had given an undertaking that the money would be used solely for the acquisition of property and for no other purpose.

Legal principle

In holding that S held the money on a trust for T under *Quistclose* principles, Lord Millett did not agree with the analysis of Lord Wilberforce that there was an initial primary trust followed by a secondary trust. What, he said, if the primary trust was not for identifiable beneficiaries but for abstract purposes? Instead, he held that the lender (T here) retains a beneficial interest in the money subject to the borrower's power (S here) to use it for the stated purposes. If he does not, as happened here to one-third of the money, then the borrower's power ceases and the resulting trust for the lender takes over and returns the money to the lender.

📖 REVISION NOTE

Twinsectra v *Yardley* is also dealt with in Chapter 12 in connection with liability for dishonestly assisting in a breach of trust. See also Chapter 10 for the problems of trusts for purposes.

 Make your answer stand out

Norris J pointed out in *Bieber* v *Teathers Ltd (in liquidation)* (2012) that 'the mere fact that the payer has paid the money to the recipient for the recipient to use it in a particular way is not of itself enough' to bring the *Quistclose* principle into play. Instead, as he pointed out, it must be clear from the terms of the transaction 'that the funds transferred should not be part of the general assets of the recipient but should be used *exclusively* to effect particular identified payments, so that if the money cannot be so used then it is to be returned to the payer'. ▶

Lord Millett put it thus in *Twinsectra* v *Yardley* (2002): 'The question in every case is whether the parties intended the money to be at the free disposal of the recipient.'

The principle in the *Quistclose* case is controversial. Why should the lender in *Quistclose* have priority? It may be mere chance that the loan is not spent as intended. If it is spent, the lender loses priority. Look at other cases on the *Quistclose* principle (e.g. *Carreras Rothmans Ltd* v *Freeman Matthews Treasure Ltd* (1985)) and at Millett (1998). Another issue is: if there is a primary express trust then who are the beneficiaries? Were they the shareholders in the *Quistclose* case? Finally, what evidence of a fiduciary relationship between S and T was there in *Twinsectra* v *Yardley*? See Hughes-Davies (2015).

📖 **REVISION NOTE**

Check the beneficiary principle in Chapters 3 and 10.

■ Putting it all together

Answer guidelines

See the essay question at the start of the chapter.

Approaching the question

This question requires you to know and understand the situations when a resulting trust arises, and then to see whether they can be linked by any coherent theory. As ever, you will not gain many marks if you just go through the situations and describe them. Instead, think about each type of trust and relate it to the theories explained at the start of this chapter.

Important points to include

For example, you could begin with the theory of Lord Browne-Wilkinson that resulting trusts can be explained on the basis of the common intention of the parties. Take a case and see whether you think that Lord Browne-Wilkinson's basis applies. Use the same approach for the 'automatic' theory of Megarry J in *Re Vandervell's Trusts (No. 2)* (1974) and Chambers' theory that they arise from lack of intention. Do not mention too many cases – five or six overall thoroughly discussed, and all raising different points, is better than twice as many dealt with superficially.

 Make your answer stand out

A really clear analysis of cases in relation to the different theories is what is required here.

READ TO IMPRESS

Buckley, R. (1994) Social security fraud as illegality. 110 *LQR* 3.

Chambers, R. (1997) *Resulting Trusts*. Oxford: Clarendon Press.

Enonchong, N. (1995) Title claims and illegal transactions. 111 *LQR* 135.

Garton, J. (2015) *Moffat's Trusts Law, Text and Materials,* 6th edn. Cambridge: Cambridge University Press.

Glister, J. (2010) Section 199 of the Equality Act 2010: how not to abolish the presumption of advancement. 73(5) *MLR* 807.

Hsaio, M. (2017) A shift in the objective deduction of secondary fact in presumption. 2 *Conv.* 101

Hughes-Davies, T. (2015) Redefining the *Quistclose* trust. 1 *Conv.* 26

Millett, P. (1998) Equity's place in the law of commerce. 114 *LQR* 214.

Swadling, W. (2008) Explaining resulting trusts. 124 *LQR* 72.

www.pearsoned.co.uk/lawexpress

 Go online to access more revision support including quizzes to test your knowledge, sample questions with answer guidelines, printable versions of the topic maps, and more!

Constructive trusts and estoppel

8

Revision checklist

Essential points you should know:

- [ ] The basis on which constructive trusts can arise
- [ ] The concept of a fiduciary
- [ ] How to identify and explain, with examples, the main situations where equity imposes a constructive trust: profits made by a fiduciary; where statute is used as an instrument of fraud; receipt of trust property by a third party
- [ ] How to identify other situations where a constructive trust has been imposed
- [ ] How to distinguish between a remedial and an institutional constructive trust
- [ ] The essential requirements for proprietary estoppel to apply
- [ ] Distinction between the effect of a proprietary estoppel and of a constructive trust

■ Topic map

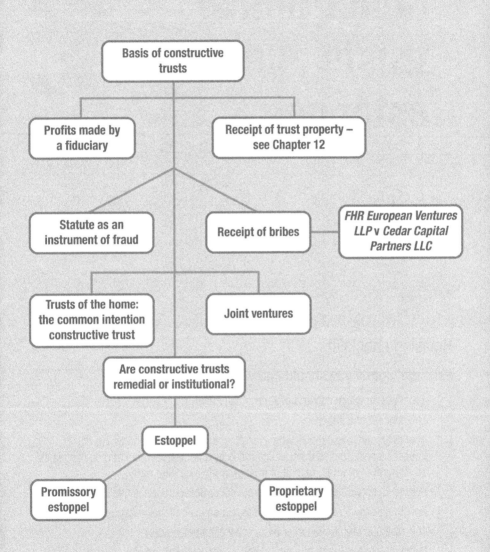

◼ Introduction

It is impossible to avoid this area in an exam paper!

You may get a straight question on it, or you will find that constructive trusts come up in other areas such as trustees, breach of trust, trusts of the family home, the nature of equity and the concept of a trust. In addition, the notion of a constructive trust appears in secret trusts (are these constructive?) and in the constitution of a trust. (Where there is a *donatio mortis causa* (DMC), this can give rise to a constructive trust.) In short, if there is one area to revise carefully, this is it. In any answer you need to be aware that there is a continuing debate about the rationale of constructive trusts. Is their development tied to the fiduciary principle or is the trust a wide-ranging remedial weapon to be used where justice demands? Read this chapter with this point in mind.

ASSESSMENT ADVICE

Essay questions

A very familiar essay question is to ask whether there is any form of words that can explain all the circumstances in which a constructive trust can arise. The answer is probably no, but you need to be able to discuss the possibilities and back up your answer with examples from the cases. This is one area where a really good knowledge of the main cases, and of any others which appeal to you, will pay dividends rather than a superficial knowledge of many cases.

Another essay scenario is to ask you to consider the difference between the institutional and the remedial constructive trust. Some of the debates here are a bit old-fashioned but still worth knowing. The case of *Binions* v *Evans* (1972) was once an absolute staple of exam questions.

Problem questions

One obvious area for a problem question is the situation where trust property has been parted with in breach of trust, and there may also be someone who has assisted in the breach. One possibility is to include a situation based on a *Boardman* v *Phipps* (1967) scenario.

◼ Sample question

Could you answer this question? Below is a typical problem question that could arise on this topic. Guidelines on answering the question are included at the end of the chapter, while a sample essay question and guidance on tackling it can be found on the companion website.

PROBLEM QUESTION

Osbert is a trustee of a family trust. The trust owns shares in the Midland Optical Illusion Co. Ltd and, at a shareholders' meeting, Osbert meets Albert, a director. Albert suggests that the company is a good investment, so Osbert buys sufficient shares to give him a controlling interest in the company. At a subsequent meeting Osbert is appointed a paid director of the company.

The company has become increasingly profitable and all of the shares have grown in value.

Advise the beneficiaries on any claims they may have against Osbert.

Constructive trusts

What are they?

KEY DEFINITION: Constructive trusts

Millett (1998) defined these as arising 'whenever the circumstances are such that it would be unconscionable for the owner of the legal title to assert his own beneficial interest and deny the beneficial interest of another'.

Note that 'constructive' does not mean that the court constructs a trust: instead it construes a trust from all the circumstances.

Can we go further than this?

Another quote is by Lord Scott in *Yeoman's Row Management Ltd* v *Cobbe* (2008):

It is impossible to prescribe exhaustively the circumstances sufficient to create a constructive trust but it is possible to recognise particular factual circumstances that will do so and also to recognise other factual circumstances that will not.

✎ EXAM TIP

Essays often ask you whether there is any all-embracing principle to explain when constructive trusts are imposed. The answer is probably no, but do not forget to include in your answer 'trusts of the home', which are dealt with later in this chapter.

All we can do here is indicate some circumstances when a constructive trust may be imposed.

■ Constructive trustees

Who are they?

In *Williams* v *Central Bank of Nigeria* (2014) the Supreme Court emphasised that there are two types:

(a) Those who have lawfully assumed fiduciary obligations in relation to trust property without a formal appointment, e.g. where there is a common intention constructive trust – see below.

(b) Those who never assumed the status of a trustee but who exposed themselves to equitable remedies by virtue of their participation in the unlawful misapplication of trust assets by dishonestly assisting in a breach of trust or knowingly receiving a trust property.

This chapter is mainly but not exclusively concerned with type (a) trustees: Chapter 12 deals with type (b) trustees. The distinction between two types of trustees is important in connection with remedies (see below under 'remedial constructive trusts') and limitation periods for actions against trustees. Actions against a type (b) trustee are subject to the six-year limit: those against type (a) trustees and also express trustees are not.

■ Profits made by a fiduciary

> **!** Don't be tempted to . . .
>
> Be sure you have a good grasp of the debate on the term 'fiduciary'. The concept of a fiduciary and a fiduciary relationship is at the very heart of equity, but attempts to define 'a fiduciary' have met with difficulty. The term certainly covers relationships other than those of trustee and beneficiary, and fiduciaries can include company directors and solicitors. A good place to start is Garton (2015: 791–805).

Note that the term '**principal**' is used to indicate a person who employs a fiduciary: it is of course a wider term than 'trustee'.

■ 'The fiduciary relationship is a concept in search of a principle' (Mason (1985)).

■ The fiduciary concept is like 'an accordion . . . it may be expanded, or compressed, to maintain the integrity of relationships perceived to be of importance to contemporary society' (Tan (1995)).

You should investigate the debate on exactly what a fiduciary means. There are certain relationships that are certainly fiduciary (e.g. trustee, solicitor to a client), but how far does it extend? Conaglen (2007) quotes (at p. 249) this definition of Finn: 'A person will be a fiduciary in his relationship with another when and insofar as that other is entitled to expect that he will act in that other's or in their joint interest to the exclusion of his own several interest.'

There is also a linked debate on what duties can be labelled as distinctively fiduciary. A starting point is Lord Herschell in *Bray* v *Ford* (1896):

> [A trustee] is not, unless expressly provided, entitled to make a profit; he is not allowed to put himself in a position where his interest and duty conflict.

 Make your answer stand out

This quotation is too often just used by students rather than analysed. There is a debate on whether there are in fact two principles: the 'no profit' principle and the 'no conflict of interest' one. There is no law against a person making a profit; the 'no profit rule' applies where a person is, as a result of their fiduciary position, in a position where duty and interest conflict. In *Boardman* v *Phipps* (below), Lord Upjohn regarded the 'no profit' principle as part of a wider 'no conflict' rule.

In the context of company directors, Vinelott J observed in *Movitex Ltd* v *Bulfield* (1988): 'I do not think that it is strictly accurate to say that a director owes a fiduciary duty to the company not to put himself in a position where his duty to the company may conflict with his personal interest or with his duty to another.'

Thus Lord Herschell's words should perhaps be rephrased to say that where there is a conflict between personal interests and duty as a trustee, then the duty is not to take advantage of that conflict and to consider only the interests of the trust. See Koh (2003).

KEY CASE

Keech v *Sandford* (1726) Sel Cas Ch 61 (Ct of Chan)

Concerning: persons in a fiduciary position must not use that position to make an unauthorised benefit for themselves

Facts

A trustee of a lease of a market was granted a renewal of the lease in his own name because the landlord did not wish to renew it on trust as the beneficiary was a minor who could not be bound by the usual covenants.

Legal principle

The trustee held the renewed lease on trust for the minor even though the trustee had neither acted fraudulently nor deprived the trust of any benefit.

KEY CASE

Boardman v *Phipps* [1967] 2 AC 46 (HL)

Concerning: same issue as in Keech v *Sandford (1726) (above), but applied in a modern context*

Facts

The trust owned a substantial holding of shares in a company and the appellants were dissatisfied with its performance. They obtained information, through this connection with the trust and acting as its agents, about the company's affairs and, as a result, they decided to obtain control of the company by purchasing the remainder of its shares. Having done this, they reorganised it and made considerable profits for themselves. The trust could not have bought the shares without seeking the sanction of the court and it did not consider doing this.

Legal principle

The appellants were held liable to account to the trust for the profits made. They were constructive trustees as they had used the trust shareholding to acquire the necessary information about the company and, in addition, the respondent beneficiary had not been kept fully informed of the situation. However, the appellants had acted in good faith throughout and so should be allowed 'liberal payment' for their skill in the negotiations which had resulted in the trust acquiring a considerable benefit.

Lord Upjohn dissented and said: 'In the long run the appellants have bought for themselves at entirely their own risk with their own money shares which the trustees never contemplated buying and they did so in circumstances fully known and approved of by the trustees.'

Thus, although the appellants made a profit, they were not in a position where there was a conflict of interest between their fiduciary duties and their personal interests. See the discussion on this in Conaglen (2007) at pages 113–25.

 Make your answer stand out

Consider the position where a fiduciary acts for two principals with potentially conflicting interests. In *Bristol and West Building Society* v *Mothew* (1998), Millett LJ emphasised the need for the informed consent of both to act. See Conaglen (2009) and also Hicks (2013) whose research has shown that the court in *Boardman* v *Phipps* recognised a proprietary constructive trust of the shares by the appellants.

KEY CASE

Queensland Mines Ltd v Hudson (1978) 18 ALR 1 (PC)

Concerning: application of the principle in Keech v Sandford (1726) and Boardman v Phipps (1967) to company directors

Facts

The defendant, the managing director of the claimant company, had obtained licences for the claimant to develop some mines. When the claimant found itself unable to do so the defendant, with the claimant's full knowledge, took the licences himself and developed them.

Legal principle

The defendant was not liable to account for profits made because he had not deprived the claimant of any opportunity and had kept the claimant fully informed. It is, however, difficult to reconcile this decision with *Boardman v Phipps* (1967) and *Regal (Hastings) Ltd v Gulliver* (1942).

Note that section 175 of the Companies Act 2006 now provides that a director must avoid acting in situations where he has an interest that conflicts, or possibly may conflict, with the interests of the company. Section 175(4)(b) provides that this duty is not infringed if the matter has been authorised by the directors. You should mention these provisions in a discussion of the above cases. Although this restates what the law was in any case, you will add to your marks by mentioning it.

 Make your answer stand out

Before you leave the question of fiduciaries and their duties, look at the approach of Conaglen (2007) whose starting point is not who can be a fiduciary but the concept of fiduciary loyalty.

Receipt of bribes and other profits acquired in breach of fiduciary duty

Lister & Co. v *Stubbs* (1890) held that a bribe received by a fiduciary from a third party was not held on trust for the principal. The reasoning was that proprietary claims (i.e. those founded on trust) were available only where there was a proprietary base for the claim i.e. the principal seeks to recover property that belonged to him before the breach of fiduciary duty. A bribe, by contrast, is not the property of the principal but is property held by the fiduciary in breach of fiduciary obligation. Here the relationship between the fiduciary and principal is that of debtor and creditor, not trustee and beneficiary.

However, this principle was reversed in *Attorney General for Hong Kong* v *Reid* (1994), which held that benefits obtained from a third party in breach of fiduciary obligation, such as bribes, belong in equity to the principal from the moment of receipt. The law was then changed by *Sinclair Investments (UK) Ltd* v *Versailles Trade Finance* (2011) to what it was before *Reid*. Now, however, the latest case approves *Reid* and overrules *Lister*.

KEY CASE

FHR European Ventures LLP v *Cedar Capital Partners LLC* **[2014] UKSC 45**

Concerning: receipt of bribes by a person in a fiduciary position

Facts

While advising F in relation to their purchase of a hotel, C had entered into an agreement with the sellers of the hotel under which C was to receive a fixed commission of £10 million for securing a purchaser. C failed to notify F of that agreement and received the commission when F bought the hotel. F sought to recover the £10 million from C.

Legal principle

The Supreme Court reiterated the general equitable rule that where an agent acquired a benefit, including as here a bribe, which came to his notice as a result of his fiduciary position, or as the result of an opportunity which results from his fiduciary position, he should be treated as having acquired the benefit on behalf of his principal, so that the benefit is beneficially owned by the principal. *Lister* v *Stubbs* was overruled and *Attorney General for Hong Kong* v *Reid* (1994) was approved. Thus, F could recover the £10 million from C. Lord Neuberger felt that this conclusion had the merit of simplicity: any benefit acquired by an agent as a result of his agency and in breach of his fiduciary duty is held on trust for the principal.

 Make your answer stand out

Read Gummow (2015) on the *FHR* decision. He points out that one reason why opinion turned against *Reid* was the rise of 'restitutionary theory' whereby any claimant had to have a proprietary base' (see above). Gummow feels that this was too restrictive an approach and he welcomes that of the Supreme Court in *FHR*.

The way in which the courts have swayed from one principle to the other in these cases can be confusing so do remember this (Figure 8.1).

Figure 8.1

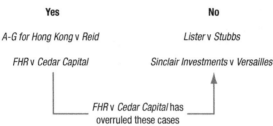

Are bribes received by an agent held on trust for the principal?

Yes	**No**
A-G for Hong Kong v *Reid*	*Lister* v *Stubbs*
FHR v *Cedar Capital*	*Sinclair Investments* v *Versailles*

FHR v *Cedar Capital* has overruled these cases

📖 **REVISION NOTE**

The above cases on receipt of bribes are yet another example of the difference between a claim under a trust as beneficiaries and under a contract as creditors. See also *Re London Wine* (Chapter 3) and *Barclays Bank* v *Quistclose* (Chapter 7). If the principal has a proprietary claim to a bribe the principal will have priority over the agent's unsecured creditors if the agent becomes insolvent. The principal will also be able to trace and follow the claim in equity (see Chapter 12).

Joint ventures

Where X and Y agree to acquire and develop land jointly and Y acquires it in his own name with the agreement of X, but then seeks to retain the land for his own benefit, the court will regard him as holding the land on trust for the joint venturers, i.e. both X and Y (*Pallant* v *Morgan* (1952)).

Statute as an instrument of fraud

See *Rochefoucauld* v *Boustead* (1897) in Chapter 4. However, the next case shows that equity does not always intervene to set aside a statutory requirement: there may be other, more important values at stake.

KEY CASE

Midland Bank Trust Co. Ltd v *Green* [1981] AC 513 (HL)

Concerning: whether a statutory requirement should be set aside as it is an instrument of fraud

Facts

An option granted by a father to his son to purchase a farm had not been registered as required by the Land Charges Act 1972 and the father, having changed his mind about the sale, then carried out a 'sham' sale to his wife so that his son's option would be defeated by this sale.

Legal principle

The son's claim failed, Lord Wilberforce observing that 'it is not fraud to rely on legal rights conferred by an Act of Parliament'.

◼ Trusts of the home: the common intention constructive trust

This is an important area for questions, and can also arise in a land law exam. The courts have used the concepts of both resulting and constructive trusts. Here is an example based on a typical exam question.

Example 8.1

Jane and her boyfriend, Tom, moved into a house which was in Jane's name as she was able to get a mortgage. However, it was always intended to be their joint home and Jane said to Tom: 'This will be our joint home for life. We will settle here.' Tom agreed and said that, as this was the case, he would pay the deposit. The house needed a great deal of renovation and Tom spent all of his spare time working on the house.

Two years later Jane met Algy and told Tom: 'Algy is the man in my life now. You will have to move out.'

Does Tom have any rights in the house?

How does the law deal with this situation?

This is an excellent study in the development of constructive trusts which could be used to illustrate an essay question. The leading cases where property is acquired in the name of one party and the other is claiming a beneficial interest, as here, are *Lloyds Bank* v *Rosset* (1991) and *Capehorn* v *Harris* (2015). Had the property been in the joint names of Jane and Tom then the issue of quantification of their respective shares under a trust would be the issue and the leading cases are Stack v *Dowden* (2007) and *Jones* v *Kernott* (2011).

If you are writing an essay on the development of the law, look also at the approach of the Court of Appeal in the 1970s under the leadership of Denning MR, based on the remedial constructive trust. *Eves* v *Eves* (1975) is a very good (and memorable) example. Is the approach in *Stack* v *Dowden* any different?

The common intention constructive trust has often been linked to proprietary estoppel in, for example, *Lloyds Bank plc* v *Rosset* (1991), where the estoppel concept of detrimental reliance was used to justify the imposition of a constructive trust. However, the prevailing orthodoxy is that the concepts of constructive trust and proprietary estoppel are different – this topic is dealt with below.

Suppose that in Example 8.1 Tom had not made any contribution or Jane had not said that the house was to be their joint home. How would Tom fare?

Law Express: *Land Law* Chapter 4 gives further details of this area, but in any discussion you could mention cases such as *Burns* v *Burns* (1984). Look at the facts and decide whether the claimant would fare any better under the tests applied in *Capehorn* v *Harris* and, if not, how the law might change to deal with her type of claim.

✓ Make your answer stand out

The Law Commission made proposals for change in this area: 'Cohabitation: The financial consequences of relationship breakdown' (Law Com. Report 307). The Government is not at present taking these proposals forward and, although a number of Private Members Bills have been introduced to give effect to them, without Government support change seems unlikely at present.

■ Are constructive trusts institutional or remedial?

A distinction is often drawn between a remedial constructive trust and an institutional one, the basis of this being that an institutional constructive trust is a trust in itself with identifiable trust property giving rise to fiduciary duties on the part of the trustee. A remedial constructive trust, by contrast, exists purely to give a remedy or to operate as a defence to some action brought by another, as in *Binions* v *Evans* (1972) where a remedial constructive trust was used to make a licence binding on a purchaser (see Law Express: *Land Law*, Chapter 5). However, it has been pointed out that in fact all constructive trusts are in essence remedial.

If you look again at cases such as *Keech* v *Sandford* and *Boardman* v *Phipps* you will see that the action was brought to obtain a remedy. Where there is a difference is that 'institutional' (for want of a better term) constructive trusts belong to recognised categories and the function of the court is merely to declare that a trust already exists. With a remedial constructive trust the trust exists only from the date of the court order when it is granted as a remedy.

There are two objections to the remedial constructive trust:

1. Looking at a constructive trust as a remedy and not as a substantive institution is wrong because, even though constructive trusts have always been remedies in one sense (see the cases above), they have also been substantive trusts because the property is trust property and, therefore, if the trustee becomes bankrupt the beneficiaries take priority over the trustee's creditors.

2. The idea of imposing a constructive trust whenever justice requires it leads to uncertainty. Mahon J memorably observed in the New Zealand case of *Carly* v *Farrelly* (1975): 'No stable system of jurisprudence can permit a litigant's claim to justice to be consigned to the formless void of individual moral opinion.'

The new remedial constructive trust was firmly rejected by the Court of Appeal in *Halifax Building Society* v *Thomas* (1995) and *Re Polly Peck International plc (No. 2)* (1998). Although it might have been given a new lease of life by the speech of Lord Scott in *Thorner* v *Major* (2009) (see below) it found no favour in the Supreme Court in *FHR European Ventures LLP* v *Cedar Capital Partners LLC* (2014). The High Court of Australia in *John Alexander's Clubs Pty Ltd* v *White City Tennis Club Ltd* (2010), while holding that on the facts there was no room for the imposition of a remedial constructive trust, still held that the concept existed and could be applied in future cases. The language of the Supreme Court in *Williams* v *Central Bank of Nigeria* (2014) could indicate that trustees in type (b) (see *Williams* v *Central Bank of Nigeria* at p. 115 above), not being true trustees, are liable to the beneficiaries under a remedial constructive trust.

This debate is fundamentally about whether a constructive trust should be tied to equitable principles, albeit functioning as a remedy in one sense, as in *Boardman* v *Phipps* (1967), or whether it should simply be a general remedy, taking its place alongside damages and injunctions (see Gardner, 2011: 275–87).

Don't be tempted to . . .

Don't just say that remedial constructive trusts are remedial without at least asking whether institutional constructive trusts are also.

■ Estoppel

KEY DEFINITION: Estoppel

This arises where one person (the representee) has been led to act on the representation of another (the representor). If so, and if the representee then acts to their detriment on the basis of this promise, then in equity the court may grant the representee a remedy.

Proprietary estoppel and promissory estoppel

Promissory estoppel applies in contractual relationships and essentially prevents a party from going back on a promise. It operates in a defensive mode.

Proprietary estoppel applies in property as well as contractual situations and can, unlike promissory estoppel, give rights where none existed before.

Although you do need to be aware of promissory estoppel, proprietary estoppel is more likely to feature in your exam as promissory estoppel is usually a topic in contract exams.

Proprietary estoppel

 Don't be tempted to . . .

Make sure that you can discuss the debate started by Lord Scott in *Yeoman's Row Management Ltd* v *Cobbe* (2008) (below) on whether estoppel should, in effect, operate only as a defence to an action and not allow an independent right to be asserted. If so, there would be no difference between promissory estoppel and proprietary estoppel.

Example 8.2

Proprietary estoppel

X owns a piece of land and says to Y: 'You can have it as a market garden.' Y takes over the land and develops it as a market garden, but the land is never conveyed to him. X later attempts to turn Y out.

Here there is no deed of conveyance, but equity provides that it could be unjust to allow a person in X's position to rely on this fact. It may therefore be remedied by the doctrine of proprietary estoppel.

✎ EXAM TIP

Note that, as estoppel is an example of equity, there is a good deal of discretion in this area and it is unwise to reach a black and white conclusion.

The nature of proprietary estoppel has been the subject of two important cases which you must be fully aware of for your exam.

✎ EXAM TIP

You may be able to use these cases as examples of the nature of equity and equitable relief and also in a discussion on unconscionability.

KEY CASE

Yeoman's Row Management Ltd v *Cobbe* [2008] UKHL 55

Concerning: estoppel: basic principles

Facts

An oral agreement between the company and Cobbe provided that a block of flats owned by the company would be demolished and Cobbe would apply for planning permission to erect houses in their place, with any excess of the proceeds over £24 million shared equally with the company. After planning permission had been obtained the company went back on the oral agreement and demanded more money. Cobbe claimed that the company was estopped from going back on the agreement.

Legal principle

Estoppel did not apply. No specific property right had been promised to Cobbe, nor would it be unconscionable for the company to go back on its assurance as Cobbe knew that only a formal contract would be binding.

Thorner v *Major* [2009] UKHL 18

Concerning: estoppel: basic principles

Facts

D had worked at P's farm for no payment from 1976 onwards, and by the 1980s he had come to hope that he might inherit the farm. No express representation had ever been made, but D relied on various hints and remarks made by P over the years, which he claimed had led him to believe that he was to inherit the farm. In addition, in 1990 P had handed D a bonus notice relating to two policies on P's life, saying: 'That's for my death duties.'

Legal principle

The handing over of the bonus notice in 1990 should not be considered alone, and the evidence had demonstrated a continuing pattern of conduct by P for the remaining 15 years of his life sufficient to amount to an estoppel.

Note that Lord Scott in effect proposed that where a future property right (as in *Thorner* v *Major*) was the subject of a representation, then the claim should be on the basis of a remedial constructive trust (see above) instead of estoppel as, when the promise was made, there was no specific property to which it could apply. The other judges, however, applied proprietary estoppel. See McFarlane (2009) for a discussion of this debate.

 Make your answer stand out

Look at more recent cases on estoppel: *Suggitt* v *Suggitt* (2012) and *Bradbury* v *Taylor* (2012) – in particular, contrast the extent of the detriment in *Thorner* v *Major* with that in *Suggitt* v *Suggitt*. See also Mee (2013). Note also the consideration of proprietary estoppel in *Southern Pacific Mortgages* v *Scott* (2014), considered in Law Express: *Land Law.* Cross-thinking between subjects really boosts your marks.

Once estoppel has been established the court must decide the remedy

The leading case here is *Jennings* v *Rice* (2002). This area, together with the effect of estoppel on third parties, is considered in more detail in Law Express: *Land Law,* Chapter 5.

Proprietary estoppel and common intention constructive trusts

You will gain extra marks in an exam if you stress the relationship between these concepts. The general view is that they operate on different principles, although they both enable a person to gain an interest in land. Lord Walker in *Stack* v *Dowden* (2007) observed that, compared with his own approach in *Yaxley* v *Gotts* (2000), 'I am now rather less enthusiastic about the notion that proprietary estoppel and "common intention" constructive trusts can or should be completely assimilated', and explained that 'Proprietary estoppel typically consists of asserting an equitable claim against the conscience of the "true" owner. The claim is a "mere equity". It is to be satisfied by the minimum award necessary to do justice. Whereas a "common intention" constructive trust, by contrast, is identifying the true beneficial owner or owners, and the size of their beneficial interests.'

Nevertheless, there is a considerable overlap, but there also seems to be an additional difference: section 2(5) of the Law of Property (Miscellaneous Provisions) Act 1989 provides that the Act does not affect the operation of resulting, implied or constructive trusts but does not mention estoppel. Thus, in *Herbert* v *Doyle* (2010) owners of two adjoining properties had verbally agreed on transfers of parking spaces on their land provided certain conditions were satisfied. Although the facts may have fitted proprietary estoppel, the court, to make the agreement enforceable, held that there was a common intention constructive trust.

However, in *Whittaker* v *Kinnear* (2011), the court held that proprietary estoppel in a case involving the sale of land *had* survived the enactment of section 2 of the Law of Property (Miscellaneous Provisions) Act 1989 and drew a distinction between domestic cases (where the party will seek an interest) and commercial cases (where the party is expecting to get a contract). An estoppel is more likely to succeed in the domestic context. *Yeoman's Row* v *Cobbe* was of course a commercial case. Note also *Matchmove Ltd* v *Dowding* (2016) which concerned one party resiling from an oral agreement for the sale of land. This was regarded by the Court of Appeal as a common intention constructive trust case and so within section 2(5) above.

 Make your answer stand out

Where there is a claim based on a constructive trust/estoppel, it might be appropriate to mention unjust enrichment. See the discussion by Lord Scott in *Yeoman's Row* v *Cobbe* of the possibility of an unjust enrichment claim in that case.

Putting it all together

Answer guidelines

See the problem question at the start of the chapter.

Approaching the question

Trustees are in a fiduciary position: you will earn marks for a careful and clear explanation of the term 'fiduciary'.

Important points to include

- Osbert has taken advantage of his position to purchase shares and obtain an appointment as fee-paying director.
- Apply case law: *Keech* v *Sandford,* and especially *Boardman* v *Phipps.* You need to contrast these with *Queensland Mines Ltd* v *Hudson.*
- It is almost certain that Osbert will hold on constructive trust.
- Will the court allow 'liberal payment' as in *Boardman*? Probably not, as here Osbert's conduct is a clearer breach than that of *Boardman.*

✓ Make your answer stand out

A thorough knowledge of *Boardman* v *Phipps* and an ability to see the contrast with *Queensland Mines Ltd* v *Hudson* is essential. Research detail on other cases.

READ TO IMPRESS

Conaglen, M. (2007) *Fiduciary Loyalty.* Oxford: Hart Publishing.

Conaglen, M. (2009) Fiduciary regulation of conflicts between duties. 125 *LQR* 111.

Dixon, M. (2005) Resulting and constructive trusts of land; the mist descends and rises. 69 *Conv.* 79.

Dixon, M. (2007) The never-ending story – co-ownership after *Stack* v *Dowden.* 71 *Conv.* 456.

Finn, P.D. (1985) *Essays in Equity.* North Ryde, NSW: Law Book Company.

Gardner, S. (1993) Rethinking family property. 109 *LQR* 263.

Gardner, S. (2011) *An Introduction to the Law of Trusts,* 3rd edn. Oxford: Oxford University Press.

Garton, J. (2015) *Moffat's Trusts Law, Text and Materials,* 6th edn. Cambridge: Cambridge University Press.

Gummow, W. (2015) Bribes and constructive trusts. 131 *LQR* 21.

Hicks, A. (2013) Proprietary relief and the order in *Boardman* v *Phipps.* 3 *Conv.* 232.

Koh, J. (2003) Once a director, always a fiduciary? 62 *CLJ* 403.

Mason, Sir A. (1985) Themes and prospects. In Finn, P. (ed.) *Essays in Equity.* Sydney: Law Book Company.

McFarlane, B. (2009) Apocalypse averted: proprietary estoppel in the House of Lords. 125 *LQR* 535.

Mee, J. (2013) Proprietary estoppel and inheritance: enough is enough? 4 *Conv.* 280.

Millett, P. (1998) Restitution and constructive trusts. 114 *LQR* 399.

Rotherham, C. (2004) The property rights of unmarried cohabitees: a case for reform. 68 *Conv.* 268.

Swadling, W. (2007) The common intention constructive trust in the House of Lords: an opportunity missed. 123 *LQR* 511.

Tan, D. (1995) The fiduciary as an accordion term: can the Crown play a different tune? 69 *ALJ* 440.

www.pearsoned.co.uk/lawexpress

 Go online to access more revision support including quizzes to test your knowledge, sample questions with answer guidelines, printable versions of the topic maps, and more!

Charitable trusts

9

Topic map

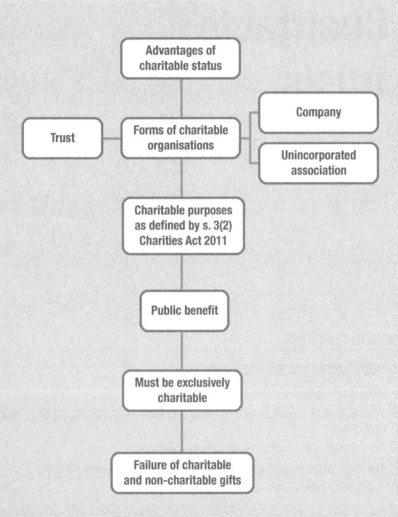

Advantages of charitable status

Forms of charitable organisations

Trust

Company

Unincorporated association

Charitable purposes as defined by s. 3(2) Charities Act 2011

Public benefit

Must be exclusively charitable

Failure of charitable and non-charitable gifts

A printable version of this topic map is available from www.pearsoned.co.uk/lawexpress

■ Introduction

This is one of the most common areas for questions in an equity exam paper.

The question may tell you that a trust is charitable so that you can concentrate on other issues, e.g. the *cy-près* doctrine. However, if it does not, you must then be aware that if the trust is not charitable you will need to apply the rules set out in Chapter 10 on non-charitable purpose trusts. Treat this chapter and Chapter 10 as aspects of one theme: how English law treats trusts for purposes.

This topic lends itself to both essay and problem questions, neither of which is too difficult, but they do require a good knowledge of case law. It is essential that you are aware of the main provisions of the Charities Act 2011. It does not change existing statute law but consolidates existing charities legislation into one statute. However, the main change to the law was made by the Charities Act 2006 and you need to make this clear in answers.

You should also look at the review of charity legislation conducted by Lord Hodgson: 'Trusted and independent: giving charity back to charities' (2012), available at: www.gov.uk/government/consultations/charities-act-2006-review. The Public Administration Select Committee (PASC) also undertook an inquiry into the impact and implementation of the 2006 Charities Act (now consolidated into the Charities Act 2011). You should look at its report, available at: www.parliament.uk. One important area considered in both reports is the current debate on what constitutes public benefit, which is considered below. The Charity Commission website (www.charity-commission.gov.uk) is an excellent place to start your research.

ASSESSMENT ADVICE

Essay questions

There are two main possible essay questions:

1. Questions on the requirement of public benefit.
2. A more general question on the Charities Acts 2006 and 2011, possibly looking at the place of charities in society in the light of the changes made by the Acts. It is essential that you look at the background to the Acts and are able to discuss the main controversial issues (e.g. the extent to which public benefit should be required for a charitable trust). ▶

Problem questions

There are two main possible problem questions:

1. Questions on whether particular objects of a trust are charitable.
2. Questions on the failure of charitable gifts.

The first area is the most likely and will require you not only to know and be able to apply the relevant part of the Charities Act, but also to discuss the extent to which cases decided under the previous law are still relevant. Select some cases and test them against the new law.

Note very precisely what the question asks you to do. It may ask you either to advise on whether the gift (often in a will) is charitable or to advise on the validity of the gift. If it is the latter, and you decide that the gift cannot be charitable, then you need to ask whether it could be valid as a private trust or, possibly, whether it comes under one of the cases where non-charitable trusts are valid.

Sample question

Could you answer this question? Below is a typical problem question that could arise on this topic. Guidelines on answering the question are included at the end of the chapter, while a sample essay question and guidance on tackling it can be found on the companion website.

PROBLEM QUESTION

Albert, by will, left the following bequests:

(a) £10,000 to the Worcester Women's Benevolent Society, which provides grants to elderly women in Worcester who are in need.

(b) £15,000 to the Faith Society, which welcomes those of any faith or none to join them in their quest for spiritual enlightenment.

(c) £20,000 to provide scholarships to enable children resident in Worcester to attend university – preference to be given to children of workers employed in the porcelain industry in Worcester.

(d) The residue of his property on trust to be used for such charitable, humanitarian or benevolent causes as his trustees may select.

Can you advise Albert's trustees on the validity of these gifts?

◾ Advantages of charitable status

This topic can appear in an essay question and you should be prepared to discuss it under two heads:

1. Legal
2. Fiscal, i.e. taxation.

As you are unlikely to be asked a detailed question on the fiscal advantages, you should concentrate on the legal ones:

1. Trusts for non-charitable purposes are generally void (see Chapter 10) as there is no one to enforce them, but the Attorney General can enforce charitable trusts and, in practice, the Charity Commissioners police the charity sector. There is scope here for a good answer that thinks laterally by linking material on both types of purpose trusts – charitable and non-charitable – and compares them from the point of view of enforceability.

2. The requirement of certainty of objects does not apply to charitable trusts. Once again you can impress the examiner with lateral thinking and draw a comparison with private trusts.

📖 **REVISION NOTE**

See, for example, *McPhail* v *Doulton* (1971) in Chapter 3.

Rules against perpetuity

✎ **EXAM TIP**

It is worth taking time to be absolutely clear about the meaning of the rules against perpetuities, as very few students do so, and it will be a real plus point for you in the exam.

The rule against inalienability does not apply to charitable trusts but it does apply to non-charitable purpose trusts (see Chapter 10).

The rule against remoteness of vesting does not apply to a gift over from one charity to another. If this takes place *beyond* the perpetuity period, then it is not affected by the rule (s. 2(2) Perpetuities and Accumulations Act 2009).

Example 9.1

In his will Jack leaves all his estate to Hanbury School, a registered charity. The first point is that, although the school may last beyond the period fixed by the rule against ▶

---

inalienability (see Chapter 10 for issues that apply to non-charitable purpose trusts), this does not affect the validity of this trust as it is charitable.

The will then provides that if the school shall ever cease to exist, any remaining funds from the estate not used shall go to the Hospital of St John.

Clearly this may take place long beyond the new 125-year perpetuity period, which deals with remoteness of vesting (see Chapter 3). Even so, the gift is valid.

✎ EXAM TIP

Take some time to master the above point. Greater detail will not be needed: just clarity about the precise point.

■ Forms of charitable organisation

This is really just background detail but it will stop you making fundamental errors. Although charity law is a part of the law of trusts (because charities were enforced by equity and not the common law), a charity can exist as:

■ a trust;

■ a company;

■ an unincorporated association, i.e. a body which is not a company and which has technically no legal existence (see Chapter 10 for more on this).

 Make your answer stand out

Look at charities in the context of their wider social purpose: as at June 2017 there were nearly 167,000 registered charities with a combined annual income of £74 billion. They are supported by more than 3.7 million volunteers. What part do they, and should they, play in our society?

■ Definition of charity

Three basic tests for charitable status exist (see Figure 9.1). See also section 2 of the Charities Act 2011 for a brief definition of charitable purposes.

Figure 9.1

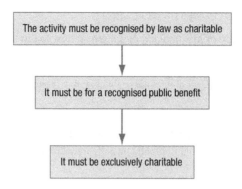

✎ **EXAM TIP**

Make sure that in a problem question you apply each of these tests to each situation.

■ Charitable purposes recognised by law

Section 3(1) of the Charities Act 2011 sets out the charitable purposes recognised by law. The following sections refer to paragraphs of section 3(1).

(a) Prevention or relief of poverty

KEY CASE

Re Coulthurst [1951] Ch 661 (HC)

Concerning: meaning of poverty in charity law

Facts

The facts of this case do not aid an understanding of the legal principle.

Legal principle

Evershed MR said that 'poverty does not mean destitution . . . it may not be unfairly paraphrased as meaning persons who have to "go short"'.

KEY CASE

Re Niyazi's Will Trusts [1978] 3 All ER 785 (HC)

Concerning: application of the meaning of poverty in charity law

Facts

A gift was left as a contribution to the cost of building a 'working men's hostel'.

Legal principle

This was charitable, even though there was no express limitation to those who were poor as the words 'working men' and 'hostel' indicated those with a lower income.

(b) Advancement of education

Exam questions often deal with trusts for research: are they educational?

KEY CASE

Re Hopkins' Will Trusts [1965] Ch 669 (HC)

Concerning: meaning of education

Facts

A trust for the promotion of research into finding the Bacon–Shakespeare manuscripts was held charitable.

Legal principle

Education must be used in a wide sense and extends beyond teaching. Research must either:

- be of educational value to the researcher; or
- pass into the store of educational material or improve the sum of communicable knowledge.

(c) Advancement of religion

Thornton v *Howe* (1862) 31 Beav 14 (Ct of Chan)

Concerning: trusts for the advancement of religion

Facts

A trust to promote the writings of Joanna Southcote, who founded a small sect and proclaimed that she was with child by the Holy Ghost and would give birth to a second Messiah, was held charitable.

Legal principle

Provided that the trust exists for the advancement of religion, the court will not say that it fails as a charity because it disapproves of its beliefs. However, note the comments of Goff J in *Church of Scientology* v *Kaufman* (1973) below.

 Make your answer stand out

The Charities Act contains an extended definition of religion to include non-deity and multi-deity groups. To what extent will this change the law, if at all? Read Hansard, 3 February and 10 February 1988, which details debates on the decision to refuse registration as a charity to the Unification Church (The Moonies). Harding (2008) has an excellent discussion in the light of the requirements of the Charities Act 2006. See also Iwobi (2009), who discusses (at p. 644) the compatibility of the charitable conception of religion with rights under the European Convention on Human Rights (ECHR) – an interesting angle that could add value to an answer.

There have been two recent Charity Commission decisions on the advancement of religion: *Re Gnostic Centre* (2009), where it was held that the trust was not charitable, and *The Druid Network* (2010), where it was held that it was. These decisions are analysed by Luxton and Evans (2011).

✎ EXAM TIP

It is a good point to note that the courts do make judgments, assisted by expert evidence, on the value of the trust in, for example, educational or religious terms. An example is Goff J in *Church of Scientology* v *Kaufman* (1973), who described the objects of the church as 'pernicious nonsense'. See, though, the *Hodkin* case on p.148.

Heads of charity

The other heads under the Charities Act 2011 are as follows. (The list begins at (d) as (a) poverty, (b) education and (c) religion have been discussed above.)

(d) Advancement of health or the saving of lives.

(e) Advancement of citizenship or community development.

(f) Advancement of the arts, culture, heritage or science.

(g) Advancement of amateur sport. (Note that sport qualifies only if it involves physical or mental skill or exertion.)

(h) Advancement of human rights, conflict resolution or reconciliation or the promotion of religious or racial harmony or equality and diversity. (See below under the discussion of political trusts.)

(i) Advancement of environmental protection or improvement.

(j) Relief of those in need by reason of youth, old age, ill health, disability, financial hardship or other disadvantage.

(k) Advancement of animal welfare.

(l) The promotion of the efficiency of the armed forces of the Crown.

(m) Other purposes currently recognised as charitable and any new charitable purposes that are similar to another charitable purpose.

 Make your answer stand out

Point out that section 3(1)(m) above enables the law on what constitutes charitable purpose to develop as society changes. This means too that you need to keep an eye out for possible new charitable purposes in future.

✎ EXAM TIP

In an exam question on the changes in the definition of charity in the Charities Act 2011, you should point out four things:

1. Many of these objects simply made a particular object specifically charitable when it was included under the general fourth head in the previous law on what constituted charitable status. This had the general title of trusts for 'other purposes beneficial to the community' and included, for example, animal welfare, which is now head (k) under the Charities Act 2011 (see above).

2. In some cases, the object formed part of an existing object and is now on its own: for example, advancement of the arts, heritage or science would previously have been listed mainly under education.

3. In some cases, the new charitable objects may go further than the existing ones (e.g. promotion of amateur sport).

4. In other cases, the law is brought into line with the current practice of the Charity Commission (e.g. new definition of religion, etc.).

✎ EXAM TIP

When revising, do not simply memorise the new heads of charity but do some deeper research into perhaps four of the heads: in a general essay question on charitable purposes there will not be time to say something useful about all of them.

Section 5 of the Charities Act 2011 makes recreational trusts charitable if they provide facilities for recreation or other leisure time activity in the interests of social welfare.

✎ EXAM TIP

If you see a mention in a question of, for example, village halls and sports centres, then it is likely that section 5 of the Charities Act 2011 will be relevant.

■ Requirement of a recognised public benefit

In an answer on this area you should refer to two areas which contain the law:

(a) The provisions of the Charities Act 2011 – see especially section 4 of the Charities Act 2011.

(b) The case law on what constitutes charitable status.

You should also refer to the guidance issued by the Charity Commission on what constitutes public benefit, but stress that this simply explains the law and does not make new law.

✓ Make your answer stand out

Point out that the public benefit requirement is relevant at two stages:

(a) When considering whether the objects are charitable at all as the courts may decide that an object is not charitable precisely through the lack of public benefit, e.g. in *Re Pinion* (1965) a testator gave his studio, pictures and certain antique furniture, etc., to be shown to the public and maintained as a collection, but the gift was not held charitable as the court observed that 'in particular the pictures   ▶

and china are quite worthless' and 'the suggestion that they should be shown in public in London or anywhere else does not bear serious consideration'. The Charity Commission calls this 'the benefit aspect'.

(b) Provided that the objects themselves are held to be for the public benefit, we need to ask whether the actual benefit is available to the public or to a section of the public. This is the aspect of public benefit considered in this section. The Charity Commission calls this 'the public aspect'.

The Charity Commission in its current guidance has recognised this distinction by issuing separate guides: one dealing with the requirement to have only charitable purposes which are for the public benefit (Public Benefit: The Public Benefit Requirement) (PB1), and then a separate guide (Public Benefit: Running a Charity) (PB2) dealing with the requirement that there must be actual benefit to the public. There is also a third guide dealing with reporting on how the trustees have carried out the charity's purposes for the public benefit (Public Benefit: Reporting) (PB3).

Some of the guidance on what is meant by benefiting the public or a sufficient section of the public is set out below, but you need to look clearly at the section on public benefit on the Charity Commission's website.

Charity Commission Guidance on the Benefit Aspect – (a) above

The Charity Commission (see PB1) points out that some charitable purposes are so obviously beneficial that there would be no need to provide further evidence, e.g. where the purpose is to provide emergency aid in the context of a natural disaster. In other cases, further evidence would be needed, e.g. of the architectural or historical merit of a building preserved under an advancement of heritage purpose.

Charity Commission Guidance on the Public Aspect – (b) above

The Charity Commission says that a charitable purpose can benefit a section of the public, but the section must be appropriate (or 'sufficient') in relation to the specific purpose. A sufficient section of the public is called a 'public class' of people. There is not a set minimum number of people who have to benefit in order to be a 'public class'. Whether a section of the public is or is not a 'public class' is not the same for every purpose. What is sufficient for one purpose may not be sufficient for another.

Special rules in trusts for the relief of poverty

Although trusts for the relief of poverty must satisfy the benefit aspect (i.e. their actual purposes must be beneficial to the public), they do not have to satisfy the public aspect.

KEY CASE

Attorney-General v *Charity Commission for England and Wales* [2012] UKUT 420 (TCC)

Concerning: the extent to which there is a requirement of public benefit in trusts for the relief of poverty

Facts

Were charities directed to the relief of poverty of restricted groups of persons charitable, given the removal of the presumption of public benefit for such charities in the Charities Act 2006?

Legal principle

The public benefit aspect of charities for the relief of poverty was provided by either the potential beneficiaries constituting a sufficient section of the public (even if a narrow class), or by a significant indirect benefit to the public as a whole arising from the relief of poverty. The effect was that the previous law contained in such decisions as *Dingle* v *Turner* (1972) was still valid.

! Don't be tempted to . . .

Say that there is no public benefit requirement in poverty cases. As you can see there is, but it differs from other cases.

As you can see from the above case, the whole area of public benefit in charity law is the subject of current debate. Lord Hodgson's report (see above) recommended that: 'No statutory definition of "public benefit" should be introduced, in order to retain the flexibility attached to the common law definition' and, although the Government stated in 2013 that it agreed with this, it also said that the possibility of change should not be completely ruled out and you should keep an eye on developments. The fundamental question is the extent to which the provisions of the Charities Act 2006 (now the 2011 Act) changed the law and you should consider two points:

- Section 4(2) of the Charities Act 2011 provides that there is no longer any presumption of public benefit. However, under the law before the Charities Act 2006 the advancement of education and religion were presumed in principle to benefit the public, although actual benefit still needed to be proved.

- Section 4(3) provides that the existing case law on what is understood to constitute public benefit shall continue to have effect. The difficulty here is that section 4(2) appears to change the law but section 4(3) provides that the law shall stay the same.

Section 14(2) provides that the Charity Commission shall promote awareness and understanding of the operation of the public benefit requirement and, in pursuit of this, it shall issue guidance under section 17. However, it has been argued that the Charity

Commission has been using this power to change the law and in *Independent Schools Council* v *Charity Commission of England and Wales and others* (2011), the Upper Chamber considered the Charity Commission's public benefit guidance in relation to independent schools. It found that the Guidance issued by the Commission – that people in poverty must not be excluded from the opportunity to benefit from a charity's work – was not an accurate statement of the law, and wider considerations apply. Although provision for the poor must go beyond just tokenistic, the trustees must decide how to treat potential beneficiaries fairly, looking at the particular circumstances of their school. The result was that the Commission withdrew its Guidance and re-issued it in its present form.

 Make your answer stand out

It has been argued that trusts for the relief of poverty, advancement of education and advancement of religion were always presumed to be charitable and so there was no need to prove that they were for the public benefit. Thus, as section 4(3) of the Charities Act 2011 expressly preserves existing case law, this should still be the position. See Hackney (2008).

Public benefit and incidental benefit

In some cases, the courts have accepted that an incidental benefit to the public is relevant in deciding whether the charitable purpose is itself for the public benefit. Consider:

- *Re Resch* (1969) – a private fee-paying hospital was held charitable as it benefited the public by reducing the need for beds in public hospitals.
- *Independent Schools Council* v *Charity Commission of England and Wales* (2011): the similar argument that independent schools promoted an indirect public benefit by relieving pressure on schools in the public sector was acknowledged as a possibility but held to be too speculative to make any difference in deciding whether the purpose was charitable.

▇ Case law on what constitutes public benefit

KEY CASE

Oppenheim v *Tobacco Securities Trust Co. Ltd* [1951] AC 297 (HL)

Concerning: public benefit in trusts for the advancement of education

Facts

A trust was set up for the education of children of employees or ex-employees of British American Tobacco.

Legal principle

This was not charitable as there was a personal connection: all the beneficiaries were connected with the same company. Lord McDermott dissented and thought that the question should be one of degree, depending on the facts of each case, and this view was supported by all of the House of Lords in *Dingle* v *Turner* (1972).

  Make your answer stand out

The decision in Oppenheim has been criticised, especially given that the company had more than 100,000 employees and the potential beneficiaries were a very large number. The actual decision may have been correct, but should have rested on a different basis: trusts of the Oppenheim kind are essentially attempts to provide tax-free fringe benefits for employees. Why should they be charitable at all?

📖 **REVISION NOTE**

The decision in *Oppenheim* v *Tobacco Securities,* where Lord Simonds made the leading speech in the House of Lords, is sometimes thought to be an example of the somewhat rigid approach which characterised equity in the 1950s and which is mentioned in Chapter 1.

KEY CASE

Re Koettgen's Will Trusts [1954] Ch 252 (HC)

Concerning: public benefit where there was a preference for a limited class

Facts

A trust for commercial education provided that preference should be given to employees of a named company of up to 75 per cent of income.

Legal principle

This was charitable, as a preference for a private group does not necessarily mean that there is no public benefit.

✎ **EXAM TIP**

This case is often used in problem questions and you should be familiar with the facts, as the problem will be given in slightly different forms. It is likely that a trust with a provision that a greater proportion of the income than in this case would go to the preferential class (e.g. 85 per cent) would not be valid.

KEY CASE

Gilmour v *Coats* [1949] AC 426 (HL)

Concerning: requirement of public benefit in trusts for the advancement of religion

Facts

A gift was left by a will to a convent of nuns who were strictly cloistered and had no contact with the outside world.

Legal principle

This was not charitable as there was no evidence of public benefit. The prayers of the nuns could not be said to benefit the public as there was no proof of this.

 Make your answer stand out

The attitude of the courts to public benefit had caused controversy, and it has been suggested that at times it was too strict. Read (Garton: 2015: 979–94), which has an excellent critique of the law. Look also at the Reports of the Charity Commission – available on its website.

One controversial case was the Charity Commission's refusal to grant charitable status to the Preston Down Trust, which runs meeting halls for the Exclusive Brethren, because the Commission was not satisfied that it had been established for the advancement of religion for public benefit, although later the Commission did grant registration. A good place to keep up with this, and other developments, is the journal *Third Sector* available at www.thirdsector.co.uk.

Political trusts

A trust that has objects that are political cannot be charitable. The reason is that it is not for the courts to decide whether what may be a controversial purpose should be for the public benefit, given the tax advantages that charities have. However, in a letter to the *Daily Telegraph* (8 August 2013), Sir Stephen Bubb, the CEO of the Association of Chief Executives of Voluntary Organisations, pointed out the long history of political campaigning by charities from the presentation of a petition to Parliament in 1787 advocating the abolition of the slave trade to the establishment of societies for the prevention of cruelty to animals in the Victorian era.

KEY CASE

McGovern v *Attorney-General* [1981] 3 All ER 493 (HC)

Concerning: trusts for political objects

Facts

Amnesty International set up a trust with these objects:

(a) relief of needy persons who were, or might be, prisoners of conscience;

(b) attempting to secure their release;

(c) abolition of torture or other inhumane methods of treatment or punishment;

(d) research into human rights.

Legal principle

Objects (a) and (d) were charitable but (b) and (c) were political as they were designed to change the policies of governments and/or change the law. Thus, the trust was not charitable.

 Make your answer stand out

This case led to much discussion (see Chesterman (1999) and look at subsequent reports of the Charity Commissioners, in particular the most recent guidance issued by the Charity Commissioners. Research the extent to which the new head of charity (h) (human rights, etc.) will enable charities to engage in activities (b) and (c) in *McGovern* (above).

Must be exclusively charitable

A gift cannot be charitable if one or more of its purposes are not charitable.

Always check for this last requirement in an exam question: it is sometimes forgotten. A good case on this point is *McGovern* v *Attorney-General* (1981) (above).

KEY CASE

Chichester Diocesan Fund and Board of Finance Inc. v *Simpson* [1944] AC 341 (HL)

Concerning: requirement that a trust must be exclusively charitable

Facts

A trust was established for 'charitable or benevolent objects'.

Legal principle

It was not exclusively charitable as the words 'or benevolent' implied that the trust existed for objects that were not charitable.

> ✎ **EXAM TIP**
>
> This case often appears in exam questions and there may be a variation to 'charitable and benevolent objects'. This will make the trust charitable as the word 'or' implies two objects, one of which (benevolent) is not charitable, but 'and' implies just one, which is charitable. However, it must be said that such nit-picking does equity little credit.

> ✎ **EXAM TIP**
>
> You will increase your marks in this area if you keep abreast of developments in other areas which could affect an application for charitable status. For example, the Supreme Court has now decided in *R (on the application of Hodkin and another)* v *Registrar General of Births, Deaths and Marriages)* (2013) that a Scientologist church can be a place of religious worship. Could this mean that Scientology will now be able to claim that it is a religious charity?

■ Failure of charitable and non-charitable gifts

A gift to a particular body, whether a charity or not, may fail because, for example:

- the body no longer exists;
- it had never existed;
- it had been amalgamated with another body.

In these cases, we need to decide where the gift goes. It could be held on a resulting trust for the donor, or the donor's estate. However, the law is reluctant, especially where the gift was intended for charitable purposes, to allow it to go away from the charitable sector, and so it is possible for the gift to be applied for similar charitable purposes under the *cy-près* doctrine.

KEY DEFINITION: *Cy-près*

'So near'.

> ✎ **EXAM TIP**
>
> This usually appears as a separate exam question and is likely to be a problem. In addition, it may involve gifts for non-charitable purposes, which is why they are also dealt with here. You may get what is, in effect, a two-part question: the first part asks you whether the gift is charitable and you are then asked to deal with the position where it has failed.

Failure of charitable gifts

Example 9.2

In his will Richard left £10,000 to his old school, Wigorn College. However, at the date of his death, the school had ceased to exist. Advise the trustees of Richard's will.

The first question is to check carefully whether the gift has actually failed. An example of where, on a close analysis, it was found not to have failed is *Re Broadbent* (2001). If the gift has failed, then ask whether the gift was for charitable purposes. The answer seems to be yes, although you can gain extra marks here for mentioning that, under the Charities Act 2011, the public benefit requirement may be tighter.

Assuming that it is, you need to discuss *cy-près* application. This will allow the gift to be applied for purposes *cy-près* (so near) (i.e. as near as possible) to the original purposes (see Figure 9.2).

Figure 9.2

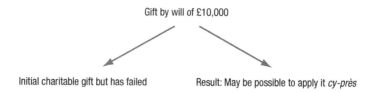

Gift by will of £10,000

Initial charitable gift but has failed   Result: May be possible to apply it *cy-près*

The result is that, returning to the example, two requirements must be satisfied:

1. The donor (Richard) must have shown a general charitable intention, i.e. to benefit not just that school but educational charity in a more general way (e.g. see *Re Rymer* (1895)). Note also *Re Harwood* (1936): it is easier to find a general charitable intention where the body had never existed at all.
2. The gift has failed within the meaning of section 62 of the Charities Act 2011.

KEY CASE

Kings v *Bultitude* **[2010] EWHC 1795 (Ch)**

Concerning: lack of a general charitable intention

Facts

A gift was left by will to the trustee of the Ancient Catholic Church 'for the general purposes of the said Church'. This church had ceased to exist at the date of the testator's death.

▶

> **Legal principle**
>
> *Cy-près* application was not possible as there was an intention to benefit only that church, and thus there was no general charitable intention.

 Make your answer stand out

See the article by Picton (2011) on this case.

If we return to the example in Figure 9.2, there is another possibility: has the school amalgamated with another school, so that that school is carrying on its purposes? If so, then it may claim the gift (see *Re Faraker* (1912)).

If the problem is that there is no general charitable intention, then *Re Slevin* (1891) may come to the rescue, as shown in Figure 9.3.

Figure 9.3

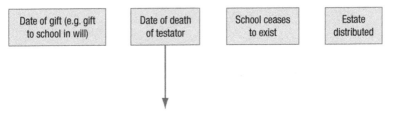

At the date this gift has been given to charity and so any lack of general charitable intention is irrelevant: *cy-près* application will follow

Thus, if the school in the above example existed at the date of Richard's death but closed before the £10,000 was paid over, no general charitable intention need be shown for *cy-près* to apply. This is known as subsequent failure.

The above discussion has assumed that the school operates as a company, which is likely because of legal liabilities. Suppose it was an unincorporated association?

📖 **REVISION NOTE**

Remember that these do not exist in law as such and this can have unfortunate consequences which we consider in Chapter 10.

However, if the gift fails because the association ceases to exist, then unincorporated association status is a positive advantage as the gift was never made to the association in any case. So, provided that its purposes are continuing, the gift can go to a body that is carrying them on. (See *Re Finger's Will Trusts* (1972).)

Failure of non-charitable gifts

Suppose that we are not dealing with a charitable gift at all. This will be the case where the purposes are not charitable, and is included in this chapter as exam questions may include situations where both charitable and non-charitable gifts fail. A particular problem is where there is a non-charitable gift to an unincorporated association as the *cy-près* rules do not apply of course. This usually arises in two situations in exams:

Situation one	Situation two
Donations are made to a disaster fund which turns out not to be charitable (e.g. see *Re Gillingham Bus Disaster Fund* (1959)). A surplus remains.	A social club, which is an unincorporated association, is wound up. (Revision point: why isn't it charitable?) What happens to the surplus? Two possibilities:
In *Re Gillingham* it was held that it went on a resulting trust for the donors, even if they could not be found.	1. It goes to the members – see *Re Bucks Constabulary Fund (No. 2)* (1979).
	2. It goes to the Crown as *bona vacantia* (e.g. see *Re West Sussex Constabulary Fund* (1970)).

Section 63 of the Charities Act 2011 allows a charity appeal to state that if the charitable purposes fail, gifts will be applied *cy-près*.

> 📖 **REVISION NOTE**
>
> Note that gifts to unincorporated associations are considered in Chapter 10.

What if there is only one member of the unincorporated association left?

KEY CASE

Hanchett–Stamford v *Attorney-General* [2008] EWHC 330 (Ch)

Concerning: assets of unincorporated associations – what happens to the assets if there is only one member left?

Facts

The claimant and her husband were the last surviving members of the Performing and Captive Animals Defence League, an unincorporated association set up to ▶

campaign for changes in the law to make performances by animals illegal where cruel methods had been used to train them. The assets amounted to £1.5 million.

Legal principle

Although the advancement of animal welfare was now a specific head of charity under the Charities Act 2011, here the objects of the organisation were political – to secure changes in the law – and therefore not charitable. Thus, the assets could not be applied *cy-près.* The court held that the last surviving member was entitled to the assets and did not agree with Walton J in *Re Buckinghamshire Constabulary Widows' and Orphans' Fund Friendly Society (No 2)* (1979), who had stated *obiter* that where there is only one member of an association left, then the association must cease to exist and the surviving member cannot claim the funds so the assets would go as *bona vacantia* to the Crown.

 Make your answer stand out

This case is another illustration of the problems caused by the failure of English law to develop a coherent rationalisation of trusts for non-charitable purposes. This area is unsatisfactory and you should consider the alternative possibilities. For a really good mark, read Chambers (1997: 61–7), who looks at the cases and analyses them from the point of view of resulting trusts.

■ Putting it all together

Answer guidelines

See the problem question at the start of the chapter.

Approaching the question

In each case, ask three questions:

1. Is the gift for charitable purposes?
2. If so, is there sufficient public benefit?
3. If so, is it exclusively charitable?

Remember: unless it is absolutely certain that the gift does not satisfy 1, you should go on to consider 2, and the same applies to 2 and 3.

Important points to include

(a) Distinguish between the two aspects of public benefit – the benefit aspect and the public aspect.

(b) Carefully explain in (a) the law on gifts for the relief of poverty and public benefit with reference to *Attorney-General* v *Charity Commission for England and Wales* (2012).

(c) Is the society in (b) for the advancement of religion? If not, could it come under other heads?

(d) The purpose in (c) is educational, but is it a public benefit? Look at *Oppenheim* and *Re Koettgen.*

(e) Is the trust in (d) exclusively charitable? *Chichester Diocesan Fund* v *Simpson.* Humanitarian?

 Make your answer stand out

In (b) adopt an imaginative approach to where the purpose could fit in.

In (c) exhibit a clear knowledge of the facts of *Re Koettgen* and knowledge of critical approaches to the law (e.g. Lord McDermott's dissenting judgment in *Oppenheim*).

READ TO IMPRESS

Chambers, R. (1997) *Resulting Trusts.* Oxford: Oxford University Press.

Chesterman, M. (1999) Foundations of charity law in the new welfare state. 62 *MLR* 333.

Garton, J. (2015) *Moffat's Trusts Law, Text and Materials,* 6th edn. Cambridge: Cambridge University Press.

Hackney, J. (2008) Charities and public benefit. 124 *LQR* 347.

Harding, M. (2008) Trusts for religious purposes and the question of public benefit. 71 *MLR* 159.

Iwobi, A. (2009) Out with the old, in with the new: religion, charitable status and the charities Act 2006. 29 *LS* 619.

Luxton, P. and Evans, N. (2011) Cogent and cohesive? Two recent Charity Commission decisions on the advancement of religion. 75 *Conv.* 144.

Picton, J. (2011) *Kings* v *Bultitude:* A gift lost to charity. 1 *Conv.* 69.

www.pearsoned.co.uk/lawexpress

Go online to access more revision support including quizzes to test your knowledge, sample questions with answer guidelines, printable versions of the topic maps, and more!

10

Non-charitable purpose trusts

Revision checklist

Essential points you should know:

- [ ] Why non-charitable purpose trusts are generally held void
- [ ] The special rules on trusts for animals and monuments and the principle in *Re Denley*
- [ ] The rules against perpetuities (in brief) and how they affect these trusts
- [ ] What unincorporated associations are and why gifts to them cause problems
- [ ] The possible solutions: trust for members or gifts to the members on a contractual basis

■ Topic map

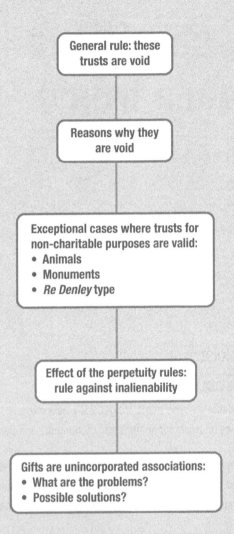

General rule: these
trusts are void

Reasons why they
are void

Exceptional cases where trusts for
non-charitable purposes are valid:
- Animals
- Monuments
- *Re Denley* type

Effect of the perpetuity rules:
rule against inalienability

Gifts are unincorporated associations:
- What are the problems?
- Possible solutions?

A printable version of this topic map is available from www.pearsoned.co.uk/lawexpress

■ Introduction

The fact that this is a complex area should not put you off answering a question on it because examiners, knowing that the topic is complex, will reward candidates who make a decent attempt at the question.

You should not attempt a question on this area without a good knowledge of charitable trusts, as your answer will require you to explain why the trust is not charitable, which is why it falls into this category.

ASSESSMENT ADVICE

Essay questions

An essay question will almost certainly focus on the reasons why non-charitable purpose trusts are generally held to be void, and so you will need good knowledge not only of the law but also of current literature in this area.

Problem questions

A problem question may involve one or more gifts and ask you to decide whether they are valid. You will need to explain why they are not valid charitable gifts, although this should not occupy too much of your time as the question is not about charity. You may decide to investigate whether the gift could take effect as a valid private trust, and here you will need to investigate whether it satisfies the rules on certainty of objects (see Chapter 3). This is well worth doing as it shows the examiner that you are thinking laterally, although do so only if there is a reasonable possibility of a valid private trust.

The other possibility is that it may be a gift to an unincorporated association, in which case the law is the same as for other non-charitable purpose trusts but will need to be approached from a different angle. In both situations you will also need to mention the application of the rule against inalienability.

■ Sample question

Could you answer this question? Below is a typical problem question that could arise on this topic. Guidelines on answering the question are included at the end of this chapter, while a sample essay question and guidance on tackling it can be found on the companion website.

PROBLEM QUESTION

John wishes to make a will under which:

1. £10,000 is left for the maintenance of his tomb in the churchyard of St Catherine's Church, Droitwich.
2. £1,000 is left for the maintenance of his dog, Hugo.
3. £20,000 is left to the Hanbury Cricket Club to build a new pavilion.
4. £50,000 is left to the Worcester branch of the XYZ Political Party.

Can you advise John on whether, and to what extent, his wishes can be carried out?

■ General rule for non-charitable purpose trusts

The general rule is that these trusts are void.

KEY CASE

Re Astor's Settlement Trusts [1952] Ch 534 (HC)

Concerning: non-charitable purpose trusts

Facts

A trust was established for various purposes, including the maintenance of good relations between nations and the preservation of the independence of newspapers.

Legal principle

The trust was void. It was for non-charitable purposes (it was not even argued that they were charitable) and there was no one who could enforce the trust.

📖 **REVISION NOTE**

Go to Chapter 9 and see why these purposes were not charitable.

This was the first time that the courts clearly held that these trusts were void. Why was this so? The best way is to set these trusts in the context of trusts in general (see Figure 10.1).

Figure 10.1

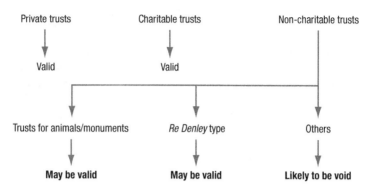

You need to remember that Figure 10.1 is only a sketch, and although various details need to be fitted in, it should guide you through this area.

A recent example of a trust being held invalid as being for non-charitable purposes is *Re St Andrew's (Cheam) Lawn Tennis Club Trust* (2012) where trustees were empowered to allow land to be used for playing tennis by persons associated with a local church. This was held not to be charitable and so invalid as a trust for non-charitable purposes.

Reasons why these trusts are void

Look at Figure 10.1 and consider the following two points:

1. A trust must have someone who can compel performance of it (the beneficiary principle).
2. The origin of this principle is in a statement of Grant MR in *Morice* v *Bishop of Durham* (1805).

 Make your answer stand out

Read Getzler J. (2012) who analyses *Morice* v *Bishop of Durham* in the light of both contemporary developments and previous case law.

How do the trusts in Figure 10.1 fare?

- A private trust can be enforced by the beneficiaries.
- A charitable trust can be enforced by the Attorney General.
- A non-charitable purpose trust has no one to enforce it.

The objects of a trust (except a charitable trust) must be expressed with sufficient certainty to enable the court to control it. This is really another way of looking at the issue raised by the beneficiary principle: the need for the court to be able to control the trust.

If the objects of the trust in *Re Astor* were not carried out, who would be able to take action? Even if there was someone to argue in court that there was a breach of these trusts, could the court tell whether this was so? If all the trust funds in *Re Astor* were being spent on the promotion of war instead of peace, then the court could no doubt find a breach, but look at some of the other cases below and see whether the court could decide if there was a breach.

The principle in *Re Astor* has been applied to:

- a trust for the purposes of a contemplative order of nuns (*Leahy* v *Attorney-General for New South Wales* (1959));
- a trust for the Labour Party (*Re Grant's Will Trusts* (1979));
- a trust to provide a useful memorial (*Re Endacott* (1960)).

In the rest of this chapter we shall refer to the *Re Astor* principle as the 'beneficiary principle'.

📖 **REVISION NOTE**

Go to Chapter 9 and look at *Gilmour* v *Coats* and note the similarity between it and *Leahy*.

 Make your answer stand out

See Chapter 1 of *Trends in Contemporary Trust Law* (Matthews, 1996). If you are aiming for an above-average mark on this question you must read further than the textbooks on the issues involved here, and this chapter is the place to start.

The way forward is now to look at:

- ways in which the courts have tried to limit the scope of the beneficiary principle;
- ways in which the beneficiary principle comes into conflict with other rules and concepts;
- ways in which the law might develop in the future.

Return to Figure 10.1. You will see that it mentions two situations where these trusts may be valid and you need to consider them in more detail.

■ Exceptions to the beneficiary principle

Trusts to care for animals and for the upkeep of specific monuments

This is an anomaly. Remember that *Re Astor* was the first case where the beneficiary principle was held to invalidate trusts for non-charitable purposes. Thus, before then, although it was realised that there were objections to them, there was some freedom for the courts to develop the law as they saw fit. This explains this exception.

Some cases are *Re Hooper* (1932) (monuments) and *Re Dean* (1889) (animals).

Note that the courts now confine these cases within narrow limits: for example, a gift to maintain an animal and also to breed from it would not be valid – breeding would take it beyond caring. This is a common examination point.

Note also *Re Endacott* (1960): this is an example of the unwillingness of the courts to extend the law.

Trusts of the *Re Denley* type

> **KEY CASE**
>
> *Re Denley's Trust Deed* [1969] 1 Ch 373 (HC)
>
> *Concerning: validity of a trust which appeared to be primarily for purposes and not persons*
>
> Facts
>
> Land was conveyed to trustees to hold it for the purpose of a recreation or sports ground, primarily for the benefit of the employees of a company and then for the benefit of such other person(s) as the trustees might allow.
>
> Legal principle
>
> The trust was valid as it was for the benefit of the employees and was not a purpose trust.

> **✎ EXAM TIP**
>
> Examiners will expect you to be able to analyse the issues in this case, so be prepared and read the judgment and the relevant articles in the 'Read to impress' section below.

Ways in which the beneficiary principle comes into conflict with other rules and concepts

Having learned the rule and the exceptions to the beneficiary principle, you now need to be able to appreciate how it comes into collision with two other areas: the perpetuity rules and gifts to unincorporated associations (see Figure 10.2).

Figure 10.2

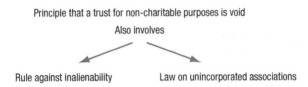

Principle that a trust for non-charitable purposes is void

Also involves

Rule against inalienability   Law on unincorporated associations

Effect of the perpetuity rules

> ### Example 10.1
>
> John leaves £1,000 to Tim on trust to care for the monument over his tombstone. When is the trust to end? When Tim dies it is possible for new trustees to be appointed, but this is not the point.

There are two perpetuity rules: one, mentioned in Chapter 3, deals with remoteness of vesting and affects trusts for individuals.

> **📖 REVISION NOTE**
>
> Go to Chapter 3 and check that you are clear on the perpetuity rule on remoteness of vesting.

The other rule, which deals with situations where the trust property can be tied up for too long, is often known as the **rule against inalienability** or the rule against indefinite duration. Section 18 of the Perpetuities and Accumulations Act 2009 provides that it does not affect 'the rule of law which limits the duration of non-charitable purpose trusts'.

KEY DEFINITION: Rule against inalienability

A gift to be held on a non-charitable purpose trust is void if it may last beyond lives or lives in being plus 21 years. (See e.g. *Leahy* v *Attorney-General for New South Wales* [1959] AC 457 for an instance of how this rule could invalidate a purpose trust.)

✎ EXAM TIP

If a question involves a purpose trust contained in a will, check when the will was executed as this date will give you the start of the perpetuity period.

In fact, the courts have tried to ensure that these trusts do not fall foul of the perpetuity period. See *Mussett* v *Bingle* (1876) regarding the assumption that a monument would be erected within the perpetuity period.

Note: *Re Haines* (1952): the courts take notice of the lifespan of particular animals; here, that a cat could not live longer than 21 years. Thus, the gift was valid.

Where a trust states that it is to last for 'as long as the law allows', this will be taken to be the perpetuity period and will therefore be valid (*Re Hooper* (1932)).

Gifts to unincorporated associations

Take a look at Figure 10.3.

Figure 10.3

Possible gift for the purposes of the Hanbury FC

! Don't be tempted to . . .

Skip over the topic of validity of gifts to unincorporated associations. This can be a difficult area in problem questions as it involves the following three areas:

1. beneficiary principle;
2. rule against perpetuities;
3. nature of unincorporated associations.

▶

Do keep each point distinct and apply them separately to the question.

The fundamental point is that unincorporated associations do not exist in law, so any gift must be for their purposes.

📖 **REVISION NOTE**

Go back to Chapter 9 and check that you are clear on the law on the disposal of the surplus funds of unincorporated associations, where the position is compared to the disposal of the funds of charities that have failed.

Example 10.2

Although Barbara may think she has made a gift to the club itself, she has not. Assuming that it is not a registered company, the club is an unincorporated association and so does not exist.

The next question is whether the club can be a charity.

📖 **REVISION NOTE**

Go to Chapter 9 and check on the purposes which can be charitable.

Under the Charities Act 2011, if the club is amateur the gift can be for charitable purposes and be valid.

Let us assume that Hanbury FC is semi-professional. Here we have a problem as the gift is for non-charitable purposes and must be held on trust, but these trusts are void. The same would apply if the gift had been made to a political party.

 Make your answer stand out

The fact that there are legal difficulties with these gifts has caused adverse comment. For instance, in *Re St. Andrews (Cheam) Lawn Tennis Club Trust* (above) the trust had existed for over 70 years without any apparent problems. A good quotation is:

> It would astonish a layman to be told that there was a difficulty in his giving a legacy to an unincorporated non-charitable society which he had or could have supported without difficulty in his lifetime.

(Brightman J in *Re Recher's Will Trusts* (1972)).

The result is that the courts have tried to find ways of making these gifts valid. There are two possibilities:

1. A gift on trust for the benefit of the members – see *Re Denley* above.
2. A gift to the members who will hold it on the basis of the contract between them contained in the rules of the association – see *Re Recher* below.

These possibilities often form part of a problem question in an exam. We need now to look at them carefully.

KEY CASE

Re Recher's Will Trusts [1972] Ch 526 (HC)

Concerning: validity of gifts to unincorporated associations

Facts

A gift was made to the London and Provincial Anti-Vivisection Society, a non-charitable association.

Legal principle

This was valid as it was a gift to the members as an addition to the funds subject to the contract between them as set out in the rules. It was not an immediate gift to the members.

Compare this with *Re Lipinski's Will Trusts* (1976).

KEY CASE

Re Horley Town Football Club; Hunt v McLaren [2006] EWHC 2386 (Ch)

Concerning: validity of gifts to unincorporated associations

Facts

The club was an unincorporated association. In 1948 the then president of the club had settled land on trust to secure a permanent endowment for the club and in 2002 the land was sold and the proceeds used to buy other land and provide sports facilities. A surplus remained and the issue was the precise basis on which the assets of the club were held.

Legal principle

The trust deed of 1948 should be interpreted as a contract-holding gift to the club members for the time being. The beneficial interest vested in the current full members and was held on a bare trust for them. This entitled them to call in a general meeting for the assets to be transferred to them as individuals. The decision follows *Re Recher* in basing the solution on contract, but the device of a trust is used to solve the problem of exactly where the legal ownership of the property lies pending any distribution between the members.

Make your answer stand out

There have not been many recent cases on this area and so a good knowledge of the above case will obviously bring extra marks in an exam. Research it. A good place to start is Luxton (2007).

But there is still a problem: the rule against inalienability.

KEY CASE

Re Grant's Will Trusts [1979] 3 All ER 359 (HC)

Concerning: application of the rule against inalienability to gifts to unincorporated non-charitable bodies

Facts

A gift was made for the purposes of the Chertsey Labour Party but the members did not control the property, nor could they gain control as the rules were subject to the jurisdiction of the National Executive of the Labour Party.

Legal principle

A gift to a non-charitable unincorporated association will fail if the members are unable to divide the gift between them, as it will have to be held for the association's purposes in perpetuity.

In *Re Horley Town Football Club* (above) the actual trust deed did define a perpetuity period but perpetuity was not a problem as the interests of the members vested immediately.

Note: another area where the apparent lack of a beneficiary could cause problems with the enforcement of a trust (although so far it seems not to have done so) is the *Quistclose* type of trust dealt with in Chapter 7. This is discussed in the article by Pawlowski and Summers (2007).

Future development of the law

> ✓ Make your answer stand out
>
> As essay questions are likely in this area, it is absolutely vital that you read widely and think about the issues. Look at the idea of these trusts having an enforcer who will be able to take action to enforce the trust. This would solve the fundamental problem posed at the start of this chapter. See Warburton (1985) and Pawlowski and Summers (2007). The latter argue for a general recognition by English law of the validity of non-charitable purpose trusts provided that certain conditions are satisfied, in particular that an enforcer is named in the trust instrument who is independent of the settlor and the beneficiaries.

Putting it all together

Answer guidelines

See the problem question at the start of this chapter.

Approaching the question

This question requires a clear knowledge of gifts which may be invalid as non-charitable purpose trusts together with the ability to recognise and apply the rule against inalienability.

Important points to include

1. Maintenance of tomb: valid in principle but note the perpetuity point. Apply the rule against inalienability. The trust is possibly valid as it is for the upkeep of a monument. However, is it void as offending the rule against inalienability?

2. Possibly valid as it is for the upkeep of a specific animal and not to breed from it. Is it void as offending the rule against inalienability though?

3. Can it be a trust for the benefit of the club members (*Re Denley*)? Or a gift to the members to be held on the basis of the contract between them (*Re Recher*)? Note the similarity with *Re Lipinski*.

▶

4. Similar issues to those in 3, but as the money is not allocated to a specific purpose there is the possibility that it may infringe the rule against inalienability. Can the members divide the gift among themselves or are they subject to control by the political party? See *Re Grant*.

 Make your answer stand out

Apply the rules in this chapter but also:

■ explain the perpetuities rule clearly – explain that in this context it is the rule against inalienability;

■ sketch in the underlying points – the beneficiary principle and the fact that in 3 and 4 these are unincorporated associations;

■ could the gift in 3 above be charitable?

READ TO IMPRESS

Brown, J. (2007) What are we to do with testamentary trusts of imperfect obligation? 71 *Conv.* 148.

Getzler J. (2012) *Morice* v *Bishop of Durham. Landmark Cases in Equity.* Oxford: Hart Publishing.

Luxton, P. (2007) *Re Horley Town Football Club.* 71 *Conv.* 274.

Matthews, P. (1996) The new trust: obligations without rights? In Oakley, A. (ed.) *Trends in Contemporary Trust Law.* Oxford: Oxford University Press.

Pawlowski, M. and Summers, P. (2007) Private purpose trusts – A reform proposal. 71 *Conv.* 445.

Warburton, J. (1985) Holding of property by unincorporated associations. 49 *Conv.* 318.

www.pearsoned.co.uk/lawexpress

 Go online to access more revision support including quizzes to test your knowledge, sample questions with answer guidelines, printable versions of the topic maps, and more!

11

Trusteeship and variation of trusts

Revision checklist

Essential points you should know:

- [ ] The rules on appointment, retirement and removal of trustees (in brief)
- [ ] The meaning of the term 'fiduciary' and its implications for trustees
- [ ] The distinction between duties and powers of trustees
- [ ] The main duties and powers
- [ ] The extent to which trustees may delegate
- [ ] The extent to which the trust instrument may exclude the liability of trustees
- [ ] Situations in which the terms of a trust may be varied

Topic map

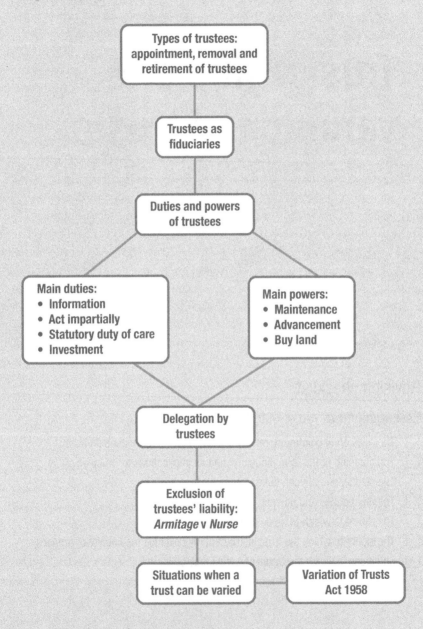

■ Introduction

The topic of trusteeship is not a difficult one but it does involve a good deal of material.

As this is a practical area, it is a good idea to familiarise yourself with an actual trust instrument to see what one looks like and be able to identify the main types of clause. There is also an interesting shift in the case law to recognising different obligations owed by fiduciaries in some types of commercial relationships from those traditionally owed. See the cases below on exclusion of liability. Note that this is not the only chapter in which trustees are considered: Chapter 8 also contained material on the fiduciary duties of trustees, and you should ensure that you are familiar with it before reading any further in this chapter.

□ REVISION NOTE

Refer back to Chapter 8 and check cases such as *Keech* v *Sandford* (1726) and *Boardman* v *Phipps* (1967). Questions on trustees often link with constructive trusts.

ASSESSMENT ADVICE

Essay questions

This is a likely area for an essay question with possibilities of questions on:

- the extent of the duties of trustees;
- the fiduciary principle, where you can use your knowledge of the constructive trust cases;
- the changes made by the Trustee Act 2000: this is a bit old hat now, but examiners may still ask it;
- the relationship between the statutory duties and powers of trustees and those in a trust instrument.

Problem questions

Questions are likely to be asked on the application of a range of duties and powers. For example, a common question examines powers of maintenance and advancement, or investment possibly combined with delegation. Do remember that the Trustee Act 1925 applies to maintenance and advancement. In this context, you should also mention the other areas governed by the Trustee Act 2000. Again, a question may bring in the ▶

scenario in *Boardman* v *Phipps* (1967) and link it with other topics which are governed by the Trustee Act 2000 (e.g. trustees' right to remuneration). In all questions, identify at the start whether a duty and/or a power is involved and state clearly the different principles applicable to the relevant one.

Sample question

Could you answer this question? Below is a typical problem question that could arise on this topic. Guidelines on answering the question are included at the end of the chapter, while a sample essay question and guidance on tackling it can be found on the companion website.

PROBLEM QUESTION

Arthur died in 2017. His will appointed Steve and Bryn as trustees of a fund worth £500,000 to hold for the benefit of Arthur's children, Kate (aged 25), Sue (aged 21) and Mary (aged 16), contingent on them reaching the age of 30.

You are asked to advise the trustees on the following:

(a) Kate, who works in an investment bank, has told them that it would be an excellent idea to invest the bulk of the fund in a company specialising in property developments in France as 'there is certain to be a property boom there next year'. If the trustees hand over the money to Kate then she is prepared to take care of the investment details.

(b) Steve thinks that it would be a good idea to invest some of the money in a small private company run by Terry, a friend of his. Terry has offered to appoint Steve as a paid director if this happens.

(c) Sue would like £70,000 of 'her money' to be paid to her now as she wishes to set up a hairdressing business. She has recently qualified as a hairdresser.

(d) Mary would like the sum of £500 to be paid to her each year so that she can receive singing lessons in Milan.

Appointment of trustees

 EXAM TIP

It is unlikely that an exam question will ask you to deal with this area in detail. However, you may get a question on the relationship between the powers contained in the trust instrument and statutory powers, so this area gives you a useful illustration.

Appointment of trustees is normally made in the first instance by the settlor or testator in the instrument or will which creates the trust. What happens later when existing trustees need to be replaced? This is where the statutory power in section 36(1) of the Trustee Act 1925 (TA 1925) applies, as it lists eight cases where trustees who die, or wish to be discharged, etc., can be replaced by the remaining trustees. In addition, appointment brings in the other element, that of control by the court, as under section 41, TA 1925, the court can appoint new trustees where it is 'impracticable or inexpedient to do so without the assistance of the court'.

■ Retirement and removal of trustees

This also involves the relationship between the statutory powers and the trust instrument although, in the case of removal, it is more likely that this will be done by the court. Retirement of trustees is governed by section 39, TA 1925, and removal is governed by the general powers of the court.

■ Trustees as fiduciaries

The topic of trustees as fiduciaries is considered in Chapter 8.

☐ REVISION NOTE

Go back to Chapter 8 and check that you are clear what a fiduciary is and look at cases where trustees have been held liable as constructive trustees as they have been in breach of their fiduciary duty. This is also a good example of where you can use the same cases to illustrate more than one point of law.

☐ REVISION NOTE

The fiduciary nature of trusteeship prevents payment of trustees unless authorised by the trust instrument or by statute – the relevant one here is section 29 of the Trustee Act 2000. Trustees are also not allowed to purchase trust property, but an exceptional case where they were is *Holder* v *Holder* (1968).

■ Duties and powers of trustees

The fundamental duty of the trustee is to execute the trust as defined in the trust instrument and in doing this to have regard to his fiduciary duty (see Chapter 8).

In the carrying out of this fundamental duty, specific duties and powers arise – see below.

- A *duty* must be exercised, although the trustee has a discretion as to precisely how it is exercised (e.g. a trustee has a duty to invest but a discretion in what to invest in).
- A *power* is discretionary but if it is a discretionary trust the trustees may be obliged to exercise a discretion.

The courts can interfere in the exercise of trustees' powers if they have acted in bad faith (*Klug* v *Klug* (1918)) but contrast in *Tempest* v *Lord Camoys* (1882) where no bad faith was shown and so the court did not interfere. Nor can the courts require trustees to give reasons for their decisions (*Re Beloved Wilkes' Charity* (1851)), but if they do give reasons for their decisions, then the court may investigate them (*Klug* v *Klug*).

KEY CASE

Pitt v *Holt* [2013] UKSC 26

Concerning: the extent of the courts' powers to control the discretionary decisions of trustees

Facts

The actual case concerned the extent to which trustees can apply to have mistakes rectified – see below.

Legal principle

Lord Walker adopted his words in *Scott* v *National Trust for Places of Historic Interest or Natural Beauty* (1998): 'Trustees must act in good faith, responsibly and reasonably. They must inform themselves, before making a decision, of matters which are relevant to the decision. These matters may not be limited to simple matters of fact but will, on occasion (indeed, quite often), include taking advice from appropriate experts, whether the experts are lawyers, accountants, actuaries, surveyors, scientists or whomsoever.'

Correcting mistakes by trustees

What is the position if trustees make a mistake?

Example 11.1

Trustees of a fund wish to exercise a power of appointment. They receive expert advice on the tax implications of this and, acting on the basis of that advice, they decide to exercise the power. Unfortunately, the advice was wrong and the tax liabilities of the trust fund and beneficiaries are considerably greater than if the advice had been correct. Who bears the liability?

In *Pitt* v *Holt* (2013) Lord Walker held in the Supreme Court that the same principle applies as above where trustees make decisions without having given proper consideration to relevant matters which they ought to have taken into consideration. He adopted this statement of Warner J in *Mettoy Pension Trustees Ltd* v *Evans* (1991): 'If the trustee has in accordance with his duty identified the relevant considerations and used all proper care and diligence in obtaining the relevant information and advice relating to those considerations, the trustee can be in no breach of duty and its decision cannot be impugned merely because in fact that information turns out to be partial or incorrect' so their decision will stand.

Thus, the fundamental issue is whether there is a breach of duty by the trustees and, if there is none, the only direct remedy available must be based on mistake, although 'there may be an indirect remedy in the form of a claim against one or more advisers for damages for breach of professional duties of care' (Lord Walker). Note *Wright v National Westminster Bank Plc* (2014) where *Pitt v Holt* was applied.

Pitt v *Holt* set aside what was known as the Rule in *Re Hastings-Bass* (1975) which said that where trustees are given a discretion and act in good faith, the court should not interfere with their actions unless it is clear that either:

(a) they would not have acted as they did had they not taken into account *irrelevant* considerations;

(b) they failed to take into account *relevant* considerations.

This was widely used in tax cases where trustees had relied on incorrect tax advice and its effect was to enable the transaction to be undone. The trustees could then, in effect, try again and exercise the power in a more tax-effective manner. In doing so they, and their professional advisers, would avoid potential liability for having acted imprudently.

📖 **REVISION NOTE**

The problem with putting the emphasis on actions against trustees is that they may be protected by an exclusion clause. See *Armitage* v *Nurse* (1998) later in this chapter.

 Make your answer stand out

The decision in *Pitt* v *Holt* has been the subject of much academic analysis and is a topical area worth looking at for exams. Look, for example, at Nolan (2013). Add to your marks by mentioning the position of Scottish law on the control of trustees – see Francis (2008).

Relationship between powers in the trust instrument and statutory powers

The legislation on trustees' powers operates in default of any provision in the trust instrument to the contrary (see s. 69(2), Trustee Act 1925). This is a useful point to explore in an essay question and is also relevant in problems (e.g. on powers of maintenance and advancement – see below).

Main duties of trustees

The duty to give information

The extent of the duty to give information to the beneficiaries is somewhat unclear and would form good material for an essay question on the extent to which trustees are accountable to the beneficiaries. There has been a shift from the approach in *Re Londonderry's Settlement* (1965), which emphasised that beneficiaries are only allowed to see documents which contain information about the trust that the beneficiaries are entitled to know and in which the beneficiaries have a proprietary interest.

In *Schmidt* v *Rosewood Trust Ltd* (2003), the court emphasised that the issue is the requirement for the court to supervise the trust.

Duty to act impartially

> **KEY CASE**
>
> *Howe* v *Earl of Dartmouth* (1802) 7 Ves 137 Chan
>
> *Concerning: duties of trustees between a life tenant and a remainderman*
>
> **Facts**
>
> The facts of this case do not aid an understanding of the legal principle.
>
> **Legal principle**
>
> The trustee must act impartially and so must strike a balance between the interests of the life tenant (income required) and the remainderman (preservation of capital required).

There are a number of rules, of which the above case is one example, that apply to decide whether investment return is payable as income to the life tenant or as capital to the remainderman. A Law Commission Report has proposed replacing these rules – see LC 315 (2009) *Capital and Income in Trusts: Classification and Apportionment*.

Statutory duty of care

This was introduced by the Trustee Act 2000 and it is vital that you read the background to this Act. The fundamental reason why it was introduced was that the duties of trustees were governed mainly by nineteenth-century case law, which was quite out of date.

KEY STATUTE

Trustee Act 2000, section 1

A trustee shall exercise such care as is reasonable having regard in particular to:

(a) any special knowledge or experience which he has or holds himself out as having;

(b) if he acts in the course of a business or profession, any special knowledge or experience which is reasonable to expect of a person acting in that business or profession.

The statutory duty of care applies to:

- investment
- acquisition of land
- appointment of agents
- insurance
- compounding of liabilities
- reversionary interests, valuations and audit.

With regard to investment the following are relevant.

KEY STATUTE

Trustee Act 2000

Section 3
A trustee may make any investment that he could make if he was absolutely entitled under the trust.

Section 4
The standard investment criteria when investing are:

(a) the suitability to the trust of particular investments;

(b) the need for diversification of investments, so far as this is appropriate.

Section 5
A trustee must obtain and consider advice about the way in which the power of investment should be exercised. Note that section 5 defines what this is and when trustees are relieved of this duty.

Cases on investment may still be useful, even if decided under the previous law (e.g. *Cowan* v *Scargill* (1985)).

■ Main powers of trustees

Powers of maintenance and advancement

As these are powers they are discretionary: see above.

You should always mention in an exam question that, by section 69(2) of the TA 1925, these can be amended or excluded by the trust instrument.

✎ EXAM TIP

Note that changes have been made to powers of maintenance and advancement where the trust is created or arises on or after 1 October 2014. This includes trusts arising under wills. Check dates in an exam question on this area.

KEY DEFINITION: Maintenance

Payment of income to beneficiaries before they are entitled.

KEY STATUTE

Trustee Act 1925, section 31

(1) Where any property is held by trustees in trust for any person whether vested or contingent, then, subject to any prior interests or charges affecting that property –

    (i)   during the *infancy* of any such person, the trustees may, at their sole discretion, pay to his parent or guardian, if any, or otherwise apply for or towards his maintenance, education, or benefit, the whole or such part, if any, of the income of that property as may, in all the circumstances, be reasonable, whether or not there is –
        (a)   any other fund applicable to the same purpose; or
        (b)   any person bound by law to provide for his maintenance or education.

Section 31 provides that the trustees shall have regard to the age of the infant and his requirements and generally to the circumstances of the case and, in particular, to what other income, if any, is applicable for the same purposes.

Under section 8 of the Inheritance and Trustees' Powers Act 2014 there are changes which give trustees complete discretion: the words 'as may, in all the circumstances, be reasonable' are replaced by 'as they shall see fit' and the section requiring the trustees to have regard to the age etc. of the infant is repealed.

Note also section 31(2): when the beneficiary reaches 18 then the trustees must pay the income to him, i.e. the discretionary power to pay maintenance ceases. It may be of course that this age is altered by the trust instrument: watch for this!

Note that the Inheritance Powers of Trustees Act merely brings the law into line with what is the common practice anyway: wills were drafted to override these provisions and those in section 32 below.

You will boost your marks in an equity exam if you cross-refer to the Supreme Court decision in *Ilott* v *Mitson* (2017) which, although primarily concerned with an award for financial provision under the Inheritance (Provision for Family and Dependants) Act 1975, also contained observations on what constitutes maintenance.

If you get a problem question on maintenance you must first consider whether the power to pay maintenance arises at all, because section 31 applies only to gifts which carry the intermediate income, i.e. give an entitlement to income before the capital is paid. One frequent instance is where there is a contingent pecuniary legacy.

Example 11.2

Sam leaves Tom by will a gift of £200,000 provided that Tom attains the age of 25. This is a legacy as it is by will, it is contingent on Tom reaching 25, and it is a gift of money so it is pecuniary.

In this case you need to apply the provisions of section 175 of the Law of Property Act 1925 to decide whether the gift carries the intermediate income.

KEY DEFINITION: Advancement

Payment of capital to beneficiaries before they are entitled.

KEY STATUTE

Trustee Act 1925

Section 32

(1) Trustees may at any time or times pay or apply any capital money (property) subject to a trust, for the advancement or benefit, in such manner as they may, in their absolute discretion, think fit, of any person entitled to the capital of the trust property or of any share thereof. . . .

There are three conditions:

(a) The amount advanced cannot exceed half of the amount to which the beneficiary is entitled. (This is often varied to allow the whole sum to be advanced.)

(b) Any sum advanced must be brought into account when capital is paid.

(c) Anyone entitled to a prior life interest must consent to the advancement.

▶

Under section 9 of the Inheritance and Trustees Powers Act the power contained to pay or apply capital is extended to the whole, rather than one-half, of the beneficiary's share in the trust fund and trustees will be able not only to pay out cash in the exercise of the statutory power of advancement but also to transfer or apply property.

KEY CASE

Re Kershaw's Trusts (1868) LR 6 Eq 322 (HC)

Concerning: meaning of advancement

Facts

An advancement was sought to enable the beneficiary's husband to set up in business and so prevent the family separating.

Legal principle

An advancement would be made. The term 'advancement' has a wider meaning than just financial benefit.

Other important cases on advancement are *Re Pilkington's Will Trust IRC* (1964) and *Re Pauling's Settle Trusts (No. 1)* (1964).

Example 11.3

Helen leaves Catherine by will a gift of £200,000 on Catherine reaching the age of 18. The will was executed on 1 September 2014. Helen died on 1 October 2014.

The date of death is the vital date in deciding if the Inheritance Powers of Trustees Act applies as it is then that the trust arises. As Helen died after the Act came into force her trustees have the power to advance the whole £200,000 to Catherine before she reaches 18.

Figure 11.1 shows a flow chart for answering questions on maintenance and advancement.

Power to buy land

This is contained in section 8, Trustee Act 2000, and gives trustees very wide powers to buy land.

Delegation by trustees

The power of trustees to delegate is contained in the following:

KEY STATUTE

Trustee Act 2000, section 11

This allows trustees to delegate all functions except:

- decisions on distribution of assets;
- decisions on whether to pay fees or other payments out of income or capital;
- appointment of new trustees;
- power to sub-delegate.

Liability for the acts of agents is now governed by the statutory duty of care in section 1, Trustee Act 2000 (above).

Figure 11.1

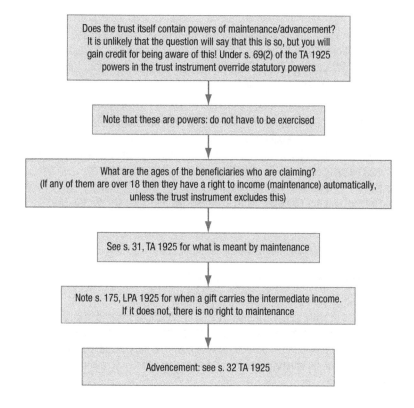

Does the trust itself contain powers of maintenance/advancement? It is unlikely that the question will say that this is so, but you will gain credit for being aware of this! Under s. 69(2) of the TA 1925 powers in the trust instrument override statutory powers

↓

Note that these are powers: do not have to be exercised

↓

What are the ages of the beneficiaries who are claiming? (If any of them are over 18 then they have a right to income (maintenance) automatically, unless the trust instrument excludes this)

↓

See s. 31, TA 1925 for what is meant by maintenance

↓

Note s. 175, LPA 1925 for when a gift carries the intermediate income. If it does not, there is no right to maintenance

↓

Advencement: see s. 32 TA 1925

■ Exclusion of trustees' liability

> **KEY CASE**
>
> *Armitage* v *Nurse* [1998] Ch 221 (HC)
>
> *Concerning: extent to which trustees can exclude liability*
>
> Facts
>
> The trust excluded the liability of the trustees for loss or damage unless caused by the actual fraud of the trustees.
>
> Legal principle
>
> This was upheld.

 Make your answer stand out

There is a view that trustee exclusion clauses have gone too far (e.g. see McCormack (1998)) and *Citibank NA* v *MBIA Assurance SA* (2006), but in *Spread Trustee Co. Ltd* v *Hutcheson* (2011) the Privy Council agreed with *Armitage* v *Nurse* that trustees can exclude liability for gross negligence.

In *Australian Securities and Investments Commission* v *Citigroup Global Markets Australia Pty Ltd* (2007) an investment bank that had advised on a takeover bid stipulated that it was not retained as a fiduciary. This was held to eliminate any liability by the bank when it traded in the shares of the company which its client proposed to take over. The case is also interesting as Jacobsen J distinguished between fiduciaries *per se* (i.e. of the kind this book has been discussing) and where there is a fiduciary relationship arising out of a specific relationship, as here (see Getzler (2008)).

■ Situations where a trust can be varied

Variation of trusts broadly means when a trustee or beneficiary wants to change the terms of the trust. Exams will focus mainly on how a trust can be varied under the Variation of Trusts Act 1958 (VTA), which gives the courts a *general* power to vary trusts, but you need to be aware of other situations where a trust can be varied to add depth to your answer.

Variation by trustees and beneficiaries

- Trustees under the trust instrument – this is unlikely to figure in the exam in detail.
- Beneficiaries under the Rule in *Saunders* v *Vautier* (1841). This usually amounts to termination of the whole trust.

Variation by the court

- Miscellaneous powers, section 57, TA 1925. This allows the court to confer extra powers in the management and administration of the trust. A good instance is wider investment powers, although now that these have been increased (see section 3, Trustee Act 2000 above) this will not be needed so often.
- Emergency powers come under the inherent jurisdiction of the court: one example is where emergency action is needed to save a building from collapse.

You must point out that the above powers do not help where the parties wish to vary the actual terms of the trust (e.g. to vary the actual beneficial interests).

- Under the VTA 1958. This gives the court a general power to vary the beneficial interests under a trust, unlike in the above situations. The court's approval is needed and in an exam question you may be asked to decide whether the court should do so. Good cases to include are: *Re Weston's Settlements* (1969), *Re CL* (1969) and *Re Remnant's Settlement Trusts* (1970). In *Re Bernstein* (2008) the court gave its approval to a tax-saving arrangement on behalf of beneficiaries whose interest was contingent on reaching the age of 25.
- In *Wright* v *Gater* (2011) one issue was whether the court should approve a postponement of vesting of the capital so that the beneficiary would receive it at the age of 30 and not 18. The court refused: there was no principle that postponement of vesting beyond the age of majority was desirable and there was nothing in the character or life of the beneficiary to suggest that there should be a postponement here.

■ Putting it all together

Answer guidelines

See the problem question at the start of this chapter.

▶

Approaching the question

This question requires you to look carefully at the duties and powers of trustees, but also to use material from Chapter 8 on fiduciaries and the personal liabilities of beneficiaries (see Chapter 12). This is a common overlap between subject areas. You should say that you assume that any trust instrument has not altered the duties and powers of the trustees.

Important points to include

(a) Begin with section 1, Trustee Act 2000 (duty of care) and consider this in the light of section 3 (general powers of investment) and section 4 (criteria when investing). Trustees can take advice from others (see s. 5, TA 2000), but is this a wise decision here? Note also that Kate is a beneficiary. See 'Personal liability of trustees and beneficiaries', Chapter 12.

(b) Possible conflict of interest, *Boardman* v *Phipps* (1967). Steve may be liable for director's fees as a constructive trustee.

(c) What was the date of Arthur's death? The question says that it was in 2017. So you will need to answer in relation to Sue and Mary on the basis that the Inheritance Powers of Trustees Act 2014 is in force.

(d) Section 32, Trustee Act 1925 (power of advancement) – but it is not her money yet. Is she asking for too much? She is entitled to one-third of £500,000 but, as s. 9 of the 2014 Act applies, all of this can be advanced subject to the overriding duty of the trustees to act in good faith after considering all the relevant circumstances. Apply cases, e.g. *Re Kershaw's Trusts* (1868).

(e) Section 31, Trustee Act 1925 (power of maintenance) – does the gift carry the intermediate income? Even so, is this a proper case for maintenance? Trustees may be committed to paying sums for years to come. Apply section 31 of the TA 1925 as amended by section 8 of the 2014 Act.

 Make your answer stand out

Clear knowledge of the provisions of the Inheritance and Powers of Trustees Act 2014 and relevant case law.

READ TO IMPRESS

Conaglen, M. (2011) Reviewing the effect of fiduciary decisions. 70(2) *CLJ* 301.

Cottrell, R. (1971) *Re Remnant's Settlement Trusts.* 34 *MLR* 98.

Davies, P. (2011) Correcting mistakes: whither the rule in *Re Hastings-Bass*. 5 *Conv.* 406.

Dunn, A. (2001) Trusting in the prudent woman of business. In Scott-Hunt, S. and Lim, H. (eds) *Feminist Perspectives on Equity and Trusts.* London: Cavendish Press.

Francis, D. (2008) Hastings-Bass and his Scottish friends. 24 *SLT* 161.

Getzler, J. (2008) Excluding fiduciary duties: the problem of investment banks. 124 *LQR* 15.

Koh, J. (2003) Once a director, always a fiduciary? 62 *CLJ* 403.

Luxton, P. (1997) Variations of trusts: settlor's intentions and the consent principle in *Saunders* v *Vautier.* 60 *MLR* 719.

McCormack, C. (1998) The liabilities of trustees for gross negligence. 62 *Conv.* 100.

Mitchell, C. (2006) Reining in the rule in Hastings-Bass. 122 *LQR* 35.

Nolan, R. (2013) Fiduciaries and their flawed decisions. 129 *LQR* 469.

Nolan, R. and Conaglen, M. (2006) Hastings-Bass and third parties. 65 *CLJ* 499.

www.pearsoned.co.uk/lawexpress

Go online to access more revision support including quizzes to test your knowledge, sample questions with answer guidelines, printable versions of the topic maps, and more!

12

Breach of trust

Revision checklist

Essential points you should know:

- [ ] When a breach of trust can arise
- [ ] The distinction between actions *in rem* and actions *in personam*
- [ ] The different meanings of the term 'breach of trust'
- [ ] The notion of taking an account and what this can lead to
- [ ] The significance of *Target Holdings Ltd* v *Redferns* (1996)
- [ ] When a person who has received trust property in breach of trust can be liable to the beneficiaries
- [ ] When a person who has assisted in a breach of trust (as distinct from receiving trust property) can be liable to the beneficiaries
- [ ] How to apply the rules governing the tracing of trust property
- [ ] The personal liability of trustees

Topic map

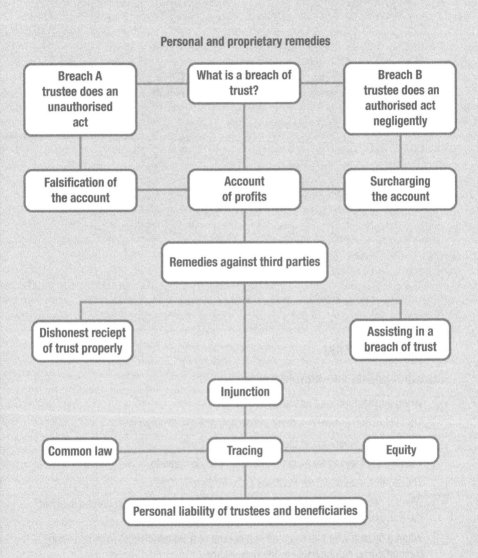

Personal and proprietary remedies

Breach A
trustee does an
unauthorised
act

What is a breach of
trust?

Breach B
trustee does an
authorised act
negligently

Falsification of
the account

Account
of profits

Surcharging
the account

Remedies against third parties

Dishonest reciept
of trust properly

Assisting in a
breach of trust

Injunction

Common law

Tracing

Equity

Personal liability of trustees and beneficiaries

A printable version of this topic map is available from **www.pearsoned.co.uk/lawexpress**

■ Introduction

This is a complex area and needs careful study. The key is understanding how the different remedies interlock.

First learn the basic rules, concentrating on what each remedy is trying to achieve and completely ignoring the details. When you are clear on this, move on. This way you will find that you are well equipped to answer a problem question and can then progress to further reading to enable you to tackle an essay question.

Important note: in this chapter we are looking at remedies against either the trustees or the trust property.

ASSESSMENT ADVICE

Essay questions

An essay question is likely to focus on the remedies available for a breach of trust. These are the following possibilities:

- ■ a general question on the different remedies;
- ■ a question on whether compensation can be awarded for a breach of trust where you will need a good knowledge of case law, in particular *Target Holdings Ltd* v *Redferns* (1996);
- ■ a detailed look at tracing: here you may be asked to compare tracing in equity with that at common law or, as below, you may be asked only to look at tracing in equity.

Problem questions

A likely question is a detailed one on following trust property where there has been a breach of trust. An example is set out below. Provided you take a logical approach you can earn very good marks here as there is usually a right or wrong answer to most points, with some areas having room for discussion so that really good students can earn extra marks. This is an area to concentrate on when revising.

■ Sample question

Can you answer this question? Below is a typical problem question that could arise on this topic. Guidelines on answering the question are included at the end of the chapter while a sample essay question and guidance on tackling it can be found on the companion website.

PROBLEM QUESTION

Joanna is a trustee of a fund set up by Anne for the benefit of her daughter, Sally. In 2012 Joanna transferred £20,000 from the trust account into her own personal account which, before the transfer, stood at £10,000. She then paid into her personal account the sum of £15,000 which she held as trustee under the will of her friend Dave.

In 2013 she withdrew £12,000 from her account to buy a racehorse, but the horse had to be put down when it fell in a race. In 2014 she withdrew a further £6,000 which she spent on tickets in a casino. She won first prize of £1,000. In 2015 she withdrew £25,000 which she spent on a vintage car. In 2016 Joanna withdrew to a monastery in Tibet. She wrote to both Sally and Dave enclosing a cheque for £1,000 for each of them and expressing remorse at what she had done. She donated all the rest of the money to the monastery. Joanna gave the car, which is now valued at £7,000, to her daughter, Millie.

Joanna has now been declared bankrupt.

Advise her trustee in bankruptcy and the beneficiaries under both trusts as to what remedies are available to them to restore the property to the trust.

■ Personal and proprietary remedies

Personal remedies are sought by an action *in personam* and proprietary remedies by an action *in rem.* There is a fundamental distinction between them.

Example 12.1

Action *in personam*

A trustee has a duty to invest the trust property, and in this example invests all of the £5 million trust fund in a small company on the advice of an inexperienced financial adviser. In fact, all of the money is lost when the company goes into liquidation. The beneficiaries are entitled to a remedy but the position is not straightforward as they may not be entitled to all of the money back. It may be that there was a reason for investing some of the money in that company, but not all of it, or it may be that, on the facts, there was no liability at all as the advice was not negligent. Whatever the outcome, the point is that the remedy is against the trustee personally (*in personam*).

Example 12.2

Action *in rem*

A trustee of money in a bank account in the name of the trust wrongfully withdraws that money and puts it in his own bank account or transfers it to another who knows that it is trust property. The beneficiaries have a straightforward remedy: the return of the money. This is a remedy *in rem*, i.e. against the thing itself: in this example, the restitution of the money.

The first stage is to identify the possible breaches of trust for which there may be a remedy.

■ What is a breach of trust?

There are two types of breaches:

(a)   Where the trustee misapplies trust money by, for instance, distributing it to the wrong person. The essence is that the trustee has done something which she must not do (Breach A).

(b)   Where the trustee, for instance, makes unauthorised investments and, in doing so, fails to show the necessary standard of care. Here the trustee has done something that they are entitled to do – make the investments – but has done it negligently (Breach B).

□ REVISION NOTE

Go back to Chapter 11 and check that you are familiar with the duties of trustees.

✎ EXAM TIP

Begin your answer to a problem question on remedies by identifying the actual breach of trust that has occurred. Few students do this, but it is the most important issue: no breach, no remedy, end of question. Of course, there will be a breach, but find it!

■ Remedies against the trustee or fiduciary

□ REVISION NOTE

Remember that these remedies can be awarded against an express trustee or a fiduciary. Revise your knowledge of the idea of a fiduciary and the two types of constructive trustee (see Chapter 8).

Where a breach of trust has occurred, the beneficiaries can require the taking of an account which will show that a sum has been misapplied.

There are then two possibilities, both of which lead to personal remedies.

Falsification of the account

This means that the sum misapplied is disallowed.

Example 12.3

Trustees of a trust for two children invest £100,000 in overseas companies although the trust specifically prohibits this. This is a type A breach. The amount is now £80,000. Technically, this £80,000 is in the account but as the investment was in breach of trust this sum is ignored and the investment is treated as having been bought with the trustees' own money and on their behalf. Thus, what is really a trust asset (the £80,000) as it was bought with trust money is treated as having been bought with the trustees' own money and so is not a trust asset and that is why we say that the account is falsified.

The court then requires the trustees to account to the trust for the full sum of £100,000 which was lost to the estate, i.e. to replace the £100,000.

Note that the term 'compensation' is misleading in this context as the beneficiaries are not compensated for harm suffered and so questions of foreseeability and remoteness have no place. Instead the claim is for performance of the trustees' obligation to deliver the assets of the trust (substitutive performance). However, the term 'compensation' is often used.

Surcharging the account

The account is surcharged where there is a type B breach where, for example, the beneficiary alleges that the trustee has not exercised due care and diligence in making an investment. The account is taken as if the trust had *actually* received what it *would* have received if the trustee had exercised due diligence. This is sometimes known as a reparation claim. Again, the term 'compensation' is misleading although often used.

Example 12.4

Trustees make an investment of £100,000 which is not strictly prohibited to them but, applying the standard investment criteria in section 4 of the Trustee Act 2000, appears to have been negligent. The investment is now worth £80,000 but had the money been properly invested it would have been worth £120,000. The account produced by the trustees is surcharged so that the trustees are liable for the difference between the two sums: £40,000.

The issue is often whether the trust fund should be reconstituted in full or whether there is only liability for the loss suffered by comparison with the position if the trustee had done as it should.

KEY CASE

Target Holdings Ltd v *Redferns* [1996] 1 AC 421 (HL)

Concerning: principles to be applied when the account is surcharged

Facts

The essence of the breach was the inadvertent paying away of trust money. Here X, solicitors, were acting for a mortgagor (borrower) and a mortgagee (lender) and received a mortgage advance on trust to release it to the mortgagor when the transfers of properties were executed. However, in breach of trust they released the money early, on the day before contracts were exchanged. In fact, the mortgagee subsequently lost money as the value of the properties had been overstated by some £1 million. The mortgagee claimed against the solicitors for this loss.

Legal principle

In assessing what should be awarded for breach of trust in commercial dealings such as this, bearing in mind that the solicitor was only a bare trustee, a trustee is liable only for losses caused by the breach and not for losses that would have occurred in any event. As the mortgage would have gone through in any case, the fact that the solicitors had released the mortgage advance early did not cause the loss of £1 million.

In *AIB Group (UK) plc* v *Mark Redler & Co Solicitors* (2014) the Supreme Court upheld the reasoning in *Target* v *Redferns* and held that in this type of case trustees are liable to the extent of the loss directly flowing from the breach of trust as determined with hindsight at the date of the trial. It is important when considering remedies to note that neither of these cases are true trusts but where a trust is only brought into operation to facilitate a commercial purpose, e.g. a mortgage advance. See Televantos and Maniscalco (2015) and note also *Creggy* v *Barnett* (2016) and the article on this case by Whayman (2017).

 Make your answer stand out

Lord Browne-Wilkinson felt in *Target* that a causal link should have had to have been proved between the loss and the breach of duty by the solicitors. However, Sir Peter Millet (later Lord Millet) in 'Equity's place in the law of commerce' (1998) disagreed. He argued that Lord Browne-Wilkinson failed to distinguish between substitutive performance (for a type A breach) and reparation claims (for a type B breach).

Target Holdings was an instance of the first type as the trustees performed their duty eventually by obtaining the mortgage securities and it is only in the second type that issues of causation are relevant. See also the judgment of Lord Reed in *AIB* v *Mark Redler* for a clear analysis of the similarities between common law damages and equitable compensation.

Account of profits

This is an alternative personal remedy against a trustee but of course is applicable only where the trustee has profits made by the wrongful use of trust property. The consequence of this remedy can actually be proprietary as the court may order that these profits are held on a constructive trust for the beneficiary.

> **☐ REVISION NOTE**
>
> Look at *Keech* v *Sandford* (Chapter 8) for an illustration of this: the lessor who had the lease renewed to himself in breach of trust was ordered to account to the infant beneficiary for any profits made from it.

■ Remedies against third parties

These can arise in two situations:

(a) against the trustee personally, e.g. where the trustee transfers trust money from the trust account into his own account;

(b) against third parties.

Third parties may be involved in a breach of trust in two ways: by actually receiving trust property or by assisting the trustee to commit a breach of trust. The tests for establishing liability in these cases are different.

(a) Dishonest receipt of trust property

Where a third party has received trust property there can be a proprietary remedy against him for its return. What, however, if he alleges that he did not know that it was trust property? In *Bank of Credit and Commerce International (Overseas) Ltd* v *Akindele* (2001), Nourse LJ held that there should be a single test of knowledge: did 'the recipient's state of knowledge . . . make it unconscionable for him to retain the benefit of the receipt?' This, he felt, would enable there to be common-sense decisions in the context of commercial transactions. It remains open to doubt whether this is so.

! Don't be tempted to . . .

Just say that the test here is one of unconscionability. Investigate what this means. In *Abou-Rahmah* v *Abacha* (2006) the Court of Appeal held that general suspicions about the conduct of the trustee are not enough to make the recipient liable for knowing receipt; instead there must be suspicions about specific matters. See especially the judgment of Arden LJ in this case.

There is another argument, that of Lord Millett in *Twinsectra Ltd* v *Yardley* (2002): 'Liability for knowing receipt is receipt based. It does not depend on fault.' The essence of this approach is that it imposes strict liability.

If a person is a volunteer (i.e. has received trust property as a gift) then he must always restore the property.

📖 REVISION NOTE

Remember the maxim: equity will not assist a volunteer (see Chapter 5).

✓ Make your answer stand out

The decision in *Farah Constructions Pty Ltd* v *Say-Dee Pty Ltd* (2002) is of great importance and the divergent approaches of the Australian courts are a perfect example of the debate that will always exist in equity. See the article by Nolan and Conaglen (2007).

(b) Liability of a person who has assisted in a breach of trust

Example 12.5

Suppose that a small charity owns a mini-bus and John, who is the chair of trustees, wants to sell it personally in breach of trust and keep the proceeds. He asked Steve, a friend, to find a buyer and it was through Steve that Jack bought it.

Here it is wrong to talk of a person like Steve as a constructive trustee as he has not received trust property; but he can be made liable in equity.

As no trust property has changed hands there cannot be a proprietary remedy here. Where the dishonest accessory has made a profit, there is the possibility of a reparation claim (see above). In *Novoship (UK) Ltd* v *Nikitin* (2014) it was held that, although the remedy of an account of profits is also available against a dishonest accessory, the extent of his liability is determined by common law principles of remoteness as although he is an equitable wrongdoer he is not subject to a pre-existing duty as a trustee is. See Campbell (2015).

There has been debate about the standard of dishonesty required. Lord Hutton in *Twinsectra Ltd* v *Yardley* (2002) said:

> The person must be dishonest and this means that his conduct must be dishonest by the ordinary standards of reasonable and honest people and *he realised* that by those standards his conduct was dishonest. [My italics]

This involves a subjective element (see italicised words above) and this has caused controversy. In *Barlow Clowes International Ltd (in liquidation)* v *Eurotrust International Ltd* (2006), the Judicial Committee of the Privy Council held that in cases of dishonest assistance in a breach of trust, a person is dishonest if he had knowledge of the elements of the transaction that rendered his participation contrary to the ordinary standards of honest behaviour. *Starglade Properties Ltd* v *Nash* (2010) is a good illustration of the operation of this principle.

 Make your answer stand out

Consider whether the decision in *Barlow Clowes* (above) has changed the law from what it was thought to be after the decision of the House of Lords in *Twinsectra* v *Yardley* (2002). Look at *Abou-Rahmah* v *Abacha* (2006), and especially the judgment of Arden LJ.

(c) Injunction to restrain a breach of trust

📖 REVISION NOTE

Injunctions are dealt with in Chapter 2.

Example 12.6

Suppose that the beneficiaries in Example 12.5 had learned in advance of John's plans to sell the mini-bus. They could have restrained him from doing this by an injunction.

(d) Tracing

KEY DEFINITION: Tracing

The term, as with restitution, is often misunderstood. It is not a remedy as such but a right to trace (i.e. follow) trust property into the hands of a person who then becomes a constructive trustee of it.

Example 12.7

Jane is trustee of the funds at her local tennis club. She takes out £5,000 from the funds and uses the money to buy a car. Can the tennis club trace its funds to her car so that the car becomes trust property and, if it wishes, could the club sell it?

Rules on tracing

Tracing at common law

This right is limited and it does not allow tracing in one of the most common cases: where the defendant has mixed the trust's money in his own bank account and then gone bankrupt.

Tracing in equity

Keep two distinct points in mind:

1. Is tracing possible?
2. If so, can it be done?

First, there are four conditions as to whether tracing is possible:

1. Existence of a fiduciary relationship.

 Make your answer stand out

The necessity for this has been criticised. Lord Millett in *Foskett* v *McKeown* (2001) said that there was no logical justification for it and the history of the rule is reviewed by Televantos (2017) who also argues that it lacks justification.

---

2. Existence of an equitable proprietary interest (e.g. that of a beneficiary).
3. Tracing would not be inequitable: see *Re Diplock* (1948).
4. Property must be in a traceable form. This means that the property must be ascertainable and this will not be so if, for example, it has been spent on a holiday.

KEY CASE

Bishopsgate Investment Management (in liquidation) v *Homan* [1995] Ch 211 (CA)

Concerning: loss of the right to trace

Facts

The facts of this case do not aid an understanding of the legal principle.

> **Legal principle**
>
> Tracing will not be permitted into an overdrawn account as, clearly, the property into which it is sought to trace has disappeared.

Second, we turn to consider whether tracing can be done.

Rules on tracing in equity

Follow through these rules. They are the ones most likely to arise in an exam.

> **✎ EXAM TIP**
>
> Problem questions will almost certainly concentrate on the position where a trustee has mixed trust money with his own.

Rule one

> **KEY CASE**
>
> *Re Hallett's Estate* (1880) 13 Ch D 696 (HC)
>
> *Concerning: withdrawals from an account*
>
> **Facts**
>
> The facts of this case do not aid an understanding of the legal principle.
>
> **Legal principle**
>
> When making withdrawals from an account, a trustee is presumed to spend his own money first. Once the amount in the account falls below the amount of trust funds, it is assumed that part of the trust funds must have been spent. Any later payments into the account are not treated as repayments of the trust money unless the trustee has shown an intention to do this (*Roscoe* v *Winder* (1915)).

Example 12.8

A trustee, Phillip, puts £10,000 of trust money and £3,000 of his own money into the trust account. He takes out £11,000 and spends it. £3,000 of this is presumed to be his own money, but the remainder must be trust money. Therefore, there is now £2,000 of trust money left. He then puts £3,000 into the account. This is presumed to be his own money unless Phillip shows an intention to repay the trust money. If he does not, then although the beneficiaries can claim the £2,000 in the account, they will have to take their place along with Phillip's other creditors in a claim for the balance.

Rule two

In *Re Oatway* (1903) it was held that if a trustee mixes his own and trust money in an account and then takes all the money and spends it on identifiable property, the beneficiaries have a first charge on this property for the recovery of the trust money.

In *FHR European Ventures LLP* v *Mankarious* (2016) a fiduciary had paid trust money into one account and its own money into another account at the same bank. It was held that the funds were not mixed and so the principle in *Re Hallett's Estate* applied and not that in *Re Oatway.*

KEY CASE

Foskett v *McKeown* [2001] 1 AC 102 (HL)

Concerning: position where the trust fund has increased in value

Facts

The facts of this case do not aid an understanding of the legal principle.

Legal principle

Lord Millett held that the beneficiary may claim either:

(a) a share in the fund in proportion to which the original trust fund bore to the mixed fund at the date when it was mixed; or

(b) he may have a lien on the fund to secure a personal claim against the fund for the return of the money (per Lord Millett).

Thus, any increase in value can be claimed under option (a) but, if the fund has decreased in value, then the beneficiaries can have a lien under option (b) for the amount that they are owed. Lord Millett reiterated this principle in *Tang* v *Tang* (2017).

Rule three

The position where mixed funds in an account represent the funds of two or more trusts, or the funds of a trust and an innocent volunteer. We are concerned here with two types of competing claim:

1. between two or more persons with a right to trace;
2. between a person with a right to trace and an innocent volunteer.

Rule in *Re Clayton* (1816)

The rule in *Re Clayton* provides that, in the case of an active continuing bank account, the trustee is regarded as having taken out of the fund whatever had been first put in: basically, 'first in, first out'.

Example 12.9

Hugh, a trustee, puts £1,000 of trust A money into a bank account on 1 June and £500 of trust B money into the same account on 2 June. There is now a total of £1,500 trust money in the account. Hugh then takes out £1,200 and, in breach of trust, spends this. As the trust A money was put in first he is presumed to have taken out all of this together with £200 of trust B money. The remaining £300 belongs to trust B.

In *Barlow Clowes International Ltd (in liquidation)* v *Vaughan* (1992) the rule in *Re Clayton* (1816) – *Clayton's Case* – was not applied to claims by investors regarding shares in the assets of a company that had managed investment plans for them. The exact date on which sums owing to individuals were paid in could have simply been by chance (e.g. delay in delivery of their letter with the money).

▦ Personal liability of trustees and beneficiaries

Note that:

- ▪ trustees can escape liability: note carefully section 61 and section 62 of the Trustee Act 1925 and also the general equitable principle; see Lowry and Edmonds (2017) who highlight the extent to which the applicability of section 61 has been argued by solicitors caught up in mortgage frauds instigated by others;
- ▪ where a beneficiary participates in, or consents to, a breach of trust, then the court may impound his/her interest so that it is available to replace any loss to the trust and so can be used to satisfy the claims of other beneficiaries who have suffered loss;
- ▪ a beneficiary who is of full age and capacity and who is in possession of all the relevant facts and freely consents to a breach of trust cannot sue in respect of it afterwards.

✎ EXAM TIP

The above points may arise in a question involving trustees (see Chapter 11).

■ Putting it all together

Answer guidelines

See the problem question at the start of the chapter.

Approaching the question

Joanna is a trustee and has committed breaches of trust. Therefore, equitable remedies are available against her. Of these, the personal remedies are of no use as she is bankrupt and therefore has no assets. So, we must turn to remedies against the trust property. Go through the conditions that must be satisfied for tracing to exist – there is an equitable proprietary interest but two conditions may not be satisfied in this case: tracing must not be inequitable and the property must be in a traceable form. If a condition does not exist, then there is no point in considering tracing further. Point out as well that tracing is not a remedy in itself but leads to a remedy – in this case a constructive trust over any property successfully traced.

Important points to include

Follow through the sequence of events:

1. Joanna deposits £20,000 from the first trust account (we will refer to this as Trust A) into her own account. Her account then stands at £30,000.

2. She then pays in £15,000 from the trust under Dave's will (Trust B). Her account now stands at £45,000.

3. She withdraws £12,000 from her account to buy a racehorse. This must come first from her own money (*Re Hallett's Estate* (1880)), which is now spent, and then probably from Trust A money (*Re Clayton* (1816) but note here *Barlow Clowes International Ltd (in liquidation)* v *Vaughan* (1992)). As the racehorse is dead the money is no longer traceable. So, there is now £33,000 in the account, made up of:

    - ■ £18,000 Trust A money (£20,000 less £2,000 spent in breach of trust)
    - ■ £15,000 Trust B money.

4. Withdrawal of £6,000 to spend in a casino: from Trust A. The prize of £1,000 may be claimed by Trust A (*Re Oatway* (1903); this sum has not been included in the final calculation, *Re Tilley's Will Trust* (1967) and *Foskett v McKeown* (2001)). There is now £27,000, of which £12,000 is left from Trust A.

5. Withdrawal of £25,000 to buy a car: this must be first from Trust A (£12,000). Trust A is now exhausted. And then £13,000 from Trust B. Now £2,000 is left of Trust B's money.

▶

6. Loss of £18,000 on the car: Trusts A and B will share rateably in any losses.

7. Money to monastery: must come from Trust B – cannot be traced? Is tracing inequitable? *Re Diplock* (1948).

8. Letter: appears to be repayment – *Roscoe v Winder* (1915).

 Make your answer stand out

Many students omit the material in the introductory paragraph. This is vital. Do include it!

READ TO IMPRESS

Campbell, C. (2015) The honest truth about dishonest assistance. 2 *Conv.* 159.

Gardner, S. (2009) Moment of truth for knowing receipt?. 125 *LQR* 30.

Gardner, S. (2011) *An Introduction to the Law of Trusts,* 3rd edn. Oxford: Oxford University Press.

Lowry and Edmonds (2017) Relieving the trustee-solicitor: a modern perspective on section 61 of the Trustee Act 1925? 133 *LQR* 223.

Millett, P. (1998) Equity's place in the law of commerce. 114 *LQR* 214.

Nolan, R. and Conaglen, M. (2007) Strict liability for receipt of misapplied trust property – confusion abounds. 66 *CLJ* 19.

Televantos, A. and Maniscalco, L. (2015) Stay on target: compensation and causation in breach of trust claims. 4 *Conv.* 348.

Televantos (2017) Losing the fiduciary requirement for equitable tracing claims. 133 *LQR* 492.

Whayman, D. (2017) More clues as to the nature of the remedy for breach of trust. 2 *Conv.* 139.

www.pearsoned.co.uk/lawexpress

 Go online to access more revision support including quizzes to test your knowledge, sample questions with answer guidelines, printable versions of the topic maps, and more!

And finally, before the exam . . .

Check your progress

☐ Look at the **revision checklists** at the start of each chapter. Are you happy that you can now tick them all? If not, go back to the particular chapter and work through the material again. If you are still struggling, seek help from your tutor.

☐ Attempt the **sample questions** in each chapter and check your answers against the guidelines provided.

☐ Go online to **www.pearsoned.co.uk/lawexpress** for more hands-on revision help:

    ☐ Try the **test your knowledge** quizzes and see whether you can score full marks for each chapter.

    ☐ Attempt to answer the **sample questions** for each chapter within the time limit and check your answers against the guidelines provided.

    ☐ Evaluate sample exam answers in **you be the marker** and see if you can spot their strengths and weaknesses.

    ☐ Use the **flashcards** to test your recall of the legal principles of the key cases and statutes you've revised and the definitions of important terms.

    ☐ Identify some of the key concepts of equity: a good start would be notice, discretion in the award of remedies, fiduciaries and unconscionability. Make sure that you can discuss them as concepts rather than just using them as terms.

    ☐ Check through all areas where there is an overlap between topics because this will help your revision. This is dealt with below.

Linking it all up

Check where there are overlaps between subject areas. (You may want to review the 'revision note' boxes throughout this book.) Make a careful note of these as knowing how one topic may lead into another can increase your marks significantly. Here are some examples:

- ✔ **Constructive trusts.** A question on the nature of equity, nature of trusts, trustees, the fiduciary relationship, trusts of the home and, of course, a question on this topic itself.
- ✔ **Trustees.** A question on constructive trusts, the fiduciary relationship and a question on this topic itself.
- ✔ **Three certainties.** A question on secret trusts, formalities, constitution and one on the three certainties.
- ✔ **Non-charitable purpose trusts.** A question on the nature of trusts, charitable trusts (problem questions often ask you about situations involving both charitable and non-charitable trusts), the nature of equity and this topic itself.
- ✔ **Equitable maxims.** Essay questions on the maxims are excellent vehicles for bringing together knowledge on various topics. For example, equity does not allow a statute to be used as an instrument of fraud: secret trusts, constructive trusts. Equity looks to the intent and not the form: secret trusts, constitution of trusts, certainty of intention. Equity does not assist a volunteer: constitution of trusts, nature of a trust.
- ✔ **Nature of equity.** This topic is such a good example and such a common exam question that a more detailed plan for bringing together different strands of the whole subject is set out below.

Knowing your cases

Make sure you know how to use relevant case law in your answers. Use the table below to focus your revision of the key cases in each topic. To review the details of these cases, refer to the particular chapter.

Key case	How to use	Related topics
Chapter 1 – Nature of equity and trusts		
Patel v *Ali*	To explain the principles on which equitable remedies can be granted.	Discretion in equity.
Walsh v *Lonsdale*	To show the effect of the Judicature Acts on the grant of equitable remedies.	Fusion between equity and common law.

Key case	How to use	Related topics
Chapter 2 – Equitable remedies and doctrines		
American Cyanamid Co. v *Ethicon Ltd (No. 1)*	To explain the principles on which the courts decide whether or not to grant an interlocutory injunction.	Injunctions.
Matila Ltd v *Lisheen Properties Ltd*	To explain when an order of specific performance may be made.	Exercise of discretion in equity.
Sky Petroleum v *VIP Petroleum*	To explain when the courts use equitable remedies to enforce contractual obligations.	Equitable remedies acting *in personam*.
Co-operative Insurance Society Ltd v *Argyll Stores (Holdings) Ltd*	To explain when specific performance of an obligation will not be granted.	Bars to specific performance.
Warner Bros Pictures Inc. v *Nelson*	To explain that an injunction can be granted if it will merely encourage performance of a contract of personal service.	Injunctions in contracts of personal service.
Craddock Bros v *Hunt*	To give an instance of the use of the remedy of rectification.	Rectification of documents.
Royal Bank of Scotland v *Etridge (No. 2)*	To explain that there are different types of undue influence.	Undue influence as an equitable remedy.
Royal Bank of Scotland v *Etridge (No. 2)*	To demonstrate knowledge of the circumstances when a lender may be affected by the undue influence/ misrepresentation of the debtor.	Recent developments in equity.
Chapter 3 – The three certainties		
Re Adams and Kensington Vestry	To give an instance of the use of the words 'in full confidence' in the creation of a trust.	Certainty of intention.
Comiskey v *Bowring-Hanbury*	To explain the need to look at all the words used to see whether a trust is created.	Certainty of intention.

▶

Key case	How to use	Related topics
Chapter 3 – The three certainties *Continued*		
Vucicevic v *Aleksic*	Looking at words in context to see if there is certainty of intention.	Certainty of intention.
Anthony v *Donges*	To illustrate when there is insufficient certainty of subject matter.	Certainty of subject matter.
Re Golay	To give an instance of how the courts have approached the construction of a trust where the word 'reasonable' is used.	Certainty of subject matter.
Curtis v *Rippon*	To set out the position where part of the property is to be held on trust and part as a gift.	Trusts and gifts.
Re London Wine Co. (Shippers) Ltd	To explain the effect on the trust where the subject matter is unascertained goods.	Certainty of subject matter.
McPhail v *Doulton*	To explain the 'individual ascertainability' test in discretionary trusts.	Certainty of objects.
Re Tuck's Settlement Trusts	To explain the position where a decision on who is to benefit from a trust is made on measurable criteria.	Power to cure uncertainty.
Re Barlow's Will Trusts	To explain the test for certainty where there is a condition precedent in a trust or gift.	Distinction between conditions precedent and discretionary trusts.
Chapter 4 – Formalities		
Rochefoucauld v *Boustead*	To explain when the courts can set aside a formality requirement.	Constructive trusts.
Grey v *IRC*	To consider a direction by a beneficiary to trustees to hold for another.	s. 53(1)(c) LPA 1925.

Key case	How to use	Related topics
Chapter 4 – Formalities *Continued*		
Vandervell v *IRC*	To consider a transfer of the legal estate where there is an existing equitable interest.	s. 53(1)(c) LPA 1925.
Re Vandervell's Trusts (No. 2)	To consider formality requirements and declarations of new trusts.	s. 53(1)(c) LPA 1925.
Oughtred v *IRC*	To consider contracts to transfer equitable interests.	Specific performance.
Re Paradise Motor Co. Ltd	To consider disclaimers of equitable interests.	s. 53(1)(c) LPA 1925.
Re Danish Bacon Co. Ltd Staff Pension Fund	To ask whether a nomination in a pension fund counts as a disposition of an equitable interest.	s. 53(1)(c) LPA 1925.
Chapter 5 – Constitution		
Choithram (T) International SA v *Pagarani*	To consider the position where a settlor declared himself a trustee.	Constitution of trusts.
Re Rose	To ask when a settlor can do all in his/her power to effect a transfer.	Constitution of trusts.
Pennington v *Waine*	To give another application of the rule in *Re Rose* above.	Unconscionability.
Zeital v *Kaye*	To instance a case where the rule in *Re Rose* did not apply.	Formalities.
Re Ralli's Will Trust	To show how a trust can be constituted indirectly.	Constitution of trusts.
Strong v *Bird*	To explain what is meant by an imperfect gift and to show how equity perfects that gift.	Executors and administrators.
Sen v *Hedley*	To demonstrate that land can be the subject of a valid *donatio mortis causa*.	Constructive trusts.

▶

Key case	How to use	Related topics
Chapter 6 – Secret and half-secret trusts		
Wallgrave v *Tebbs*	To explain the rules on communication of secret trusts.	Half-secret trusts.
Re Keen	To explain that the rules on communication of secret and half-secret trusts differ.	Secret and half-secret trusts.
Re Stead	To set out the rules on communication of a secret trust where there is more than one trustee.	Joint tenants and tenants in common.
Chapter 7 – Resulting trusts		
Prest v *Petrodel Resources Ltd*	When a resulting trust arises on a voluntary transfer.	Resulting trusts
Tinsley v *Milligan*	To explain the effect, if any, of fraudulent conduct on claims to a beneficial interest in property.	Resulting trusts.
Barclays Bank Ltd v *Quistclose Investments Ltd*	To consider the position in equity where a loan is made for a specific purpose which fails.	Contrast contracts and trusts.
Re Farepak Food and Gifts Ltd (in administration)	To look at the application of the *Quistclose* principle.	Express trusts, resulting trusts, constructive trusts.
Twinsectra v *Yardley*	Nature of *Quistclose* trusts	Quistclose trusts.
Chapter 8 – Constructive trusts and estoppel		
Keech v *Sandford*	To explain the fundamental principle applicable to fiduciaries.	Constructive trusts.
Boardman v *Phipps*	To show the application of the principle in *Keech* v *Sandford* in a modern context.	Legal position of company directors.
Queensland Mines Ltd v *Hudson*	To demonstrate the limits of the principle in *Keech* v *Sandford.*	Accounts of profits.

Key case	How to use	Related topics
Chapter 8 – Constructive trusts and estoppel *Continued*		
FHR European Ventures LLP v Cedar Capital Partners LLC	A principal has a beneficial interest in a bribe acquired by an agent through his fiduciary position.	Constructive trusts and remedies for breach of trust.
Midland Bank Trust Co. Ltd v Green	To show the flexibility of equity in its application of principles.	Constructive trusts and formal requirements.
Yeoman's Row Management Ltd v Cobbe	To set out the fundamental principles applicable to proprietary estoppel.	Unconscionability.
Thorner v Major	To show that a representation for an estoppel can be a continuing one rather than an express representation.	Requirements for an estoppel.
Chapter 9 – Charitable trusts		
Re Coulthurst	To explain the meaning of 'poverty' in charity law.	Charitable purposes recognised in law.
Re Niyazi's Will Trusts	To explain the meaning of 'poverty' in charity law.	Charitable purpose recognised in law.
Re Hopkins' Will Trusts	To explain when research can be charitable.	Advancement of education.
Thornton v Howe	To set out the approach of the courts in deciding when trusts for the advancement of religion are charitable.	Charitable purposes recognised in law.
Attorney-General v Charity Commission for England and Wales	To explain the extent to which public benefit is required in trusts for the relief of poverty.	Guidance issued by the Charity Commission on public benefit and the fact that the Charities Act 2006 (now 2011) did not change the law in this area.

Key case	How to use	Related topics
Chapter 9 – Charitable trusts *Continued*		
Oppenheim v *Tobacco Securities Trust Co. Ltd*	To evaluate the requirement of public benefit in trusts for the advancement of education.	Public benefit in charitable trusts.
Re Koettgen's Will Trusts	To develop an answer on public benefit in charitable trusts following from a discussion of *Oppenheim*.	Public benefit in charitable trusts for education.
Gilmour v *Coats*	To evaluate the requirement of public benefit in trusts for the advancement of religion.	Public benefit in charitable trusts.
McGovern v *Attorney-General*	To set out criteria to help decide whether a trust exists for political purposes.	Political purposes and charity.
Chichester Diocesan Fund and Board of Finance Inc. v *Simpson*	To illustrate the principle that to be charitable a trust must be exclusively charitable.	Requirements for charitable status.
Kings v *Bultitude*	To explain that there can be no *cy-près* application of a gift where there is no general charitable intention.	Failure of charitable gifts.
Hanchett–Stamford v *Attorney-General*	To explain what happens to the assets of an unincorporated association where there is only one member left.	Charitable trusts. *Cy-près* doctrine. Non-charitable purpose trusts.
Chapter 10 – Non-charitable purpose trusts		
Re Astor's Settlement Trusts	To explain that in general trusts for non-charitable purposes are void.	Non-charitable purpose trusts.
Re Denley's Trust Deed	To explain that it may be possible to hold that what appears to be a trust for purposes can be construed as a trust for individuals.	Charitable trusts. Express private trusts.

Key case	How to use	Related topics
Chapter 10 – Non-charitable purpose trusts *Continued*		
Re Recher's Will Trusts	To explain how a gift to an unincorporated association may be valid on the basis of a contract between the members.	Non-charitable purpose trusts.
Re Horley Town Football Club	To show how the validity of a gift to an unincorporated association was decided on the contract basis of *Re Recher* but that this was combined with a trust.	Charitable trusts. Non-charitable purpose trusts.
Re Grant's Will Trusts	To illustrate how the rule against inalienability made a gift to an unincorporated association void.	Rule against inalienability. Gifts to unincorporated associations.
Chapter 11 – Trusteeship and variation of trusts		
Pitt v *Holt*	To explain the principles on which: (a) the courts can control the discretionary decisions of trustees (b) trustees' mistakes can be corrected by the courts.	Trustees' duties and powers.
Howe v *Earl of Dartmouth*	To illustrate the duty of trustees to be impartial between the beneficiaries.	Law Commission Report Capital and Income in Trusts: Classification and Apportionment.
Re Kershaw's Trusts	To show the circumstances in which the power of advancement can be exercised.	Powers of trustees.
Armitage v *Nurse*	To explain the circumstances when trustees can exclude liability.	Duties and powers of trustees.
Chapter 12 – Breach of trust		
Target Holdings Ltd v *Redferns (a firm)*	To explain the principles to be applied when assessing compensation for breach of trust.	Negligence in the administration of a trust.

▶

Key case	How to use	Related topics
Chapter 12 – Breach of trust *Continued*		
Bishopsgate Investment Management (in liquidation) v Homan	To give an instance of when the right to trace will be lost.	Tracing in equity.
Re Hallett's Estate	To explain that when making withdrawals from an account a trustee is presumed to spend his own money first.	Tracing in equity.
Foskett v McKeown	To set out the principles which apply when a fund has increased in value.	Tracing in equity.

■ Sample question

Below is an essay question that incorporates overlapping areas of the law. See whether you can answer this question by drawing upon your knowledge of the whole subject area. Guidelines on answering this question are included at the end of this section.

ESSAY QUESTION

'The function of the common law is to establish rules to govern the generality of cases . . . The function of equity is to restrain or restrict the exercise of legal rights and powers in particular cases, whenever it would be unconscionable for them to be exercised to the full.'

Watt, *Trusts and Equity* (2003)

Consider and illustrate the above statement by reference to the nature and application of modern equity.

Answer guidelines

Approaching the question

The question asks about modern equity, so no marks at all for history. Do look through the whole of this book and choose points that you can use to illustrate this answer. For example, you could choose material in Chapter 1 on the nature of equity and Chapter 8 on constructive trusts, but make your own choice.

Important points to include

- Deal with the common law point: is it true to say that it is concerned only with generalities? Generally, yes. For example, consideration in contract applies across the whole range of contracts, but with the duty of care in negligence there are variations. There is no need for much detail on common law, but show that you can contrast the two systems.

- Contrast equity and deal with the exact points raised.

- There are two of these:

    (a) Does equity operate to restrict or restrain legal rights and powers?

    (b) Is the basis of its jurisdiction unconscionability?

- In both cases it can be suggested that the statement oversimplifies:

    (a) Equity is not just about seeking to prevent injustice occurring in the application of legal rules.

    (b) Equitable jurisdiction is not just about restraining unconscionability.

Now back up these points with specific examples chosen from chapters in this book. Your choice! But do make sure that you tie your points together in a theme related to (a) and (b) above. An answer which reads like (and is) a collection of disjointed points will get a very poor mark. A useful tip is to make the first sentence of one paragraph follow on from the last sentence of the preceding one.

 Make your answer stand out

A clear analysis of terminology is needed. For instance, what is meant by 'unconscionability' and 'principle'? Look at the 'Read to impress' section at the end of Chapter 1 for sources.

▓ Further practice

To test yourself further, try to answer these three questions, which also incorporate overlapping areas of the law. Evaluate your answers using the answer guidelines available on the companion website at **www.pearsoned.co.uk/lawexpress**

Question 1

'140 years after the Judicature Act 1873, the stitching together of the common law and equity still causes problems at the seams.' Lord Toulson in *AIB Group (UK) plc* v *Mark Redler & Co Solicitors* (2014)

Critically consider this statement in the context of equitable remedies generally and remedies for breach of trust in particular.

Question 2

'The concept of the trust is an essential mechanism in enabling many activities in our society to run smoothly.'

Evaluate this statement by reference to the purposes and activities for which trusts are used.

Question 3

Distinguish between express trusts on the one hand and resulting and constructive trusts on the other. To what extent is it true to say that they have few common features and are essentially different types of legal concept?

Glossary of terms

The glossary is divided into two parts: key definitions and other useful terms. The key definitions can be found within the chapter in which they occur, as well as in the glossary below. These definitions are the essential terms that you must know and understand in order to prepare for an exam. The additional list of terms provides further definitions of useful terms and phrases which will also help you to answer examination and coursework questions effectively. These terms are highlighted in the text as they occur but the definition can only be found here.

▊ Key definitions

Advancement	Payment of capital to beneficiaries before they are entitled.
Bare trustee	A trustee with no active duties and so can be given directions by the beneficiary to transfer the legal estate.
Beneficiaries	Those for whom the property is held in trust and who therefore have an equitable interest in the property.
Constitution of a trust	A trust is constituted when the legal title to the trust property is vested in the trustee(s). A trust is unconstituted when the legal title to the trust property is not vested in the trustees.
Constructive trusts	Defined by Millett ('Equity's Place in the Law of Commerce' (1998) 114 *LQR* 214) as arising 'whenever the circumstances are such that it would be unconscionable for the owner of the legal title to assert his own beneficial interest and deny the beneficial interest of another'.
Cy-près	So near (i.e. allows property to be used for charitable purposes so near to the original ones where these have failed).
Discretionary trust	Where the trustees have a discretion as to whether a person will be a beneficiary or not.
Estoppel	Arises when the representee has been led to act on the representation of the representor. If the representee then acts to

	their detriment on the basis of this promise, then in equity the court may grant them a remedy.
Fixed trusts	Where the interests in the trust property are fixed in the trust instrument.
Half-secret trusts	Where the will or other document discloses the existence of the trusts but not the details.
Injunction	An order requiring a party either to do or not to do a particular act.
Maintenance	Means payment of income to beneficiaries before they are entitled.
Marriage consideration	In equity this includes the husband and wife and the issue of the marriage.
Misrepresentation	An untrue statement of fact which induces a person to enter into a transaction.
Notice	A purchaser is bound by an equitable interest unless he/she had either actual notice of the equitable interest of the beneficiaries or constructive notice or imputed notice.
Rectification	Where a written instrument (e.g. a contract) does not accord with the actual intentions of the parties it can be made to do so by an order of rectification.
Rescission	This remedy restores the parties to their position before the contract or other transaction was made.
Resulting trust	The beneficial interest results to, or jumps back to, the settlor who created the trust. The basis of an action founded on a resulting trust is therefore that one is seeking to recover one's own property.
Rule against inalienability	A gift to be held on a non-charitable purpose trust is void if it may last beyond lives or lives in being plus 21 years.
Rule against remoteness of vesting	Section 5 of the Perpetuities and Accumulations Act 2009 provides for a period of 125 years, which overrides any different provision in the trust instrument. However, section 16 of this Act inserts a new section 5A into the Perpetuities and Accumulations Act 1964 which provides that the new period will not apply to a will executed before the 2009 Act comes into force. Here the former rule will apply which provides that a period of 80 years could be specified.
Rule for certainty of objects in discretionary trusts	Can it be said with certainty that any given individual is or is not a member of the class? (Individual ascertainability test.)
Rule for certainty of objects in fixed trusts	All the beneficiaries must be capable of being listed, i.e. there must be no doubt as to who the beneficiaries are.

Secret trusts	Where the will or other document does not disclose the existence of the trust.
Settlor	The creator of the trust which is created by the settlor transferring property to the trustees to hold on trust or alternatively declaring that he/she is the trustee. If the trust is created by will then the trust is created by the testator.
Specific performance (SP)	An order requiring the performance of obligations under a contract. Whereas injunctions are generally negative (you must not), SP is positive (you must).
Tracing	A right to trace (i.e. follow) trust property into the hands of a person who then becomes a constructive trustee of the property.
Trust	'A trust is a relationship which arises when property is vested in a person (or persons) called the trustees, which those trustees are obliged to hold for the benefit of other persons called the *cestuis que trust* or beneficiaries' (Hanbury and Martin (2015) *Modern Equity,* 20th edn., p. 41).
Volunteer	A person who has not provided any consideration for a promise.

◾ Other useful terms

Administrator	Person(s) appointed by the court to administer the estate of a person who has died intestate.
Bona vacantia	Vacant goods, so ownership goes to the Crown.
Executor	Person(s) nominated to act in a fiduciary capacity in the carrying out of a testator's will.
Inter vivos	Between the living.
Intestate	Where a person dies without leaving a valid will.
Principal	A person who employs a fiduciary.
Will	Written document duly executed, setting out the manner in which the testator's property is to be distributed on his/her death. (Note: it is possible to have a valid oral will in the cases of those serving in the armed forces in time of war and those serving at sea.)

Index

Note: **Emboldened** entries refer to those appearing in the Glossary